Critical Acclaim for Books by Gen and Kelly Tanabe

Authors of *Get Free Cash for College, The Ultimate Scholarship Book* and *How to Write a Winning Scholarship Essay*

"Upbeat, well-organized and engaging, this comprehensive tool is an exceptional investment for the college-bound."
—*Publishers Weekly*

"A present for anxious parents."
—Mary Kaye Ritz, *The Honolulu Advertiser*

"Helpful, well-organized guide, with copies of actual letters and essays and practical tips. A good resource for all students."
—*KLIATT*

"Upbeat tone and clear, practical advice."
—*Book News*

"Unlike other authors, the Tanabes use their experiences and those of other students to guide high school and college students and their parents through the scholarship and financial aid process."
—*Palo Alto Daily News*

"What's even better than all the top-notch tips is that the book is written in a cool, conversational way."
—*College Bound Magazine*

"A 'must' for any prospective college student."
—*Midwest Book Review*

"Invaluable information ranging from the elimination of admission myths to successfully tapping into scholarship funds."
—Leonard Banks, *The Journal Press*

"The Tanabes literally wrote the book on the topic."
–*Bull & Bear Financial Report*

"Offers advice on writing a good entrance essay, taking exams and applying for scholarships and other information on the college experience–start to finish."
–*Town & Country Magazine*

"Tanabe, an expert on the application process, can discuss such topics as how to get into the college of your choice, ways to finance your college education, applying online and what universities are looking for in a student."
–*Asbury Park Press*

"Filled with student-tested strategies."
–Pam Costa, *Santa Clara Vision*

"The first book to feature the strategies and stories of real students."
–*New Jersey Spectator Leader*

1001 Ways to Pay for College

Ninth Edition

Gen and Kelly Tanabe

Harvard graduates and award-winning authors of
*Get Free Cash for College, The Ultimate Scholarship
Book* and *How to Write a Winning Scholarship Essay*

1001 Ways to Pay for College (Ninth Edition)
By Gen and Kelly Tanabe
Published by SuperCollege, LLC
2713 Newlands Avenue, Belmont, CA 94002
650-618-2221
www.supercollege.com

ISBN 13: 978-1-61760-149-1

Manufactured in the United States of America
10 9 8 7 6 5 4 3 2 1

Library of Congress Cataloging-in-Publication Data

Names: Tanabe, Gen S., author. | Tanabe, Kelly Y., author.
Title: 1001 ways to pay for college : strategies to maximize college savings, financial aid, scholarships and grants / Gen and Kelly Tanabe.
Other titles: One thousand one ways to pay for college | One thousand and one ways to pay for college
Description: Ninth edition. | Belmont, CA : SuperCollege, [2019] | Includes index.
Identifiers: LCCN 2018057199 | ISBN 9781617601491 (pbk. : alk. paper)
Subjects: LCSH: College costs--United States. | Student aid--United States. | Scholarships--United States. | Student loans--United States.
Classification: LCC LB2337.4 .T35 2019 | DDC 378.3/80973--dc23
LC record available at https://lccn.loc.gov/2018057199

CONTENTS AT A GLANCE

TABLE OF CONTENTS

This book is the culmination of more than 15 years of research and work. It has benefited from countless students, parents, financial aid officers and scholarship judges that we have met. Their insight and knowledge were invaluable.

We would like to dedicate this book to these people. And to you, our dear reader, we hope you will use the lessons in this book to make your college dreams possible.

ONE

The Many Ways To Pay For College

There's More Than One Way To Pay For College

The acceptance letter that you've been waiting for finally arrives. You tear it open and jump up and down with excitement—you've been accepted! All those months of hard work filling out applications and writing essays have paid off. You're ready to pack your bags and head for your future. There's just one thing stopping you.

The tuition bill.

When we got into college, we thought the only way to pay for it was from our (and our parents') own wallets. Unfortunately, we learned that these wallets weren't as fat as we imagined and so we were forced to look elsewhere. What we found amazed us. It turned out there were a lot of ways to pay for college besides from our own pocket.

We focused most of our energies on finding and winning scholarships. Together we won over $100,000 in scholarships, which went a long way toward paying for Harvard. Unfortunately, even that amount of money only covered half of what it would cost for four years of college. In addition to scholarships, we also turned to campus jobs, summer internships, tax breaks, asking the college for more money, creative

savings strategies and careful budgeting. It was through a combination of these efforts that we were able to ultimately graduate from Harvard debt-free.

Our experience was just one of 1,000 possible ways that enterprising students pay for college. From lucrative dorm room enterprises to taking advantage of loan repayment programs to volunteer work that pays for college, there are literally thousands of ways that you can make college affordable.

In this book we present what we consider to be the top 1001 ways to pay for college. In our experience, the reason most families feel so stressed about paying for school is not so much a lack of money but rather a lack of knowledge of the resources available. So in the following pages we present the best ways to pay for school. Some of the ways you may have heard of but never really understood, while others may be totally new.

We know that you'll learn a lot in this book, but we also hope that you'll be inspired by the options you discover. We want this book to jump-start your thinking and get you excited about taking advantage of the many opportunities that exist.

The majority of the strategies in this book are appropriate for all students. It doesn't matter if you're a high school student starting college, a college or graduate school student halfway done or an adult going back to school–you'll find strategies and ideas to help you pay for college. Of course, if you're a parent of a student and your wallet isn't as fat as your child imagines, then this book is for you, too.

Here are just a few examples of what you'll find inside. You'll learn how to:

- Find the best scholarships **#1**
- Double your scholarship dollars **#232**
- Win money from contests only open to students **#332**
- Find guaranteed scholarships **#380**
- Pay in-state tuition even if you are an out-of-state student **#383**
- Get rebates for college every time you shop **#385**
- Grow your money with a Coverdell Education Savings Account **#388**
- Maximize your 529 Savings Plan **#403**
- Prepay your education at today's prices with a pre-paid tuition plan **#408**
- Invest strategically for college **#468**
- Claim your $2,500 American Opportunity tax credit **#480**
- Take advantage of your $2,000 Lifetime Learning credit **#482**
- Deduct student loan interest from your taxes **#487**

- Get the most financial aid you deserve **#493**
- Ask for more financial aid **#536**
- Safeguard your money from financial aid scams **#543**
- Get the state to pay for your education **#556**
- Select the best student loan **#620**
- Put your loan payments on hold **#625**
- Have your student loan forgiven **#639**
- Have the military pay for your education **#700**
- Save the money you already have **#750**
- Make your college cheaper **#783**
- Attend a tuition-free college **#790**
- Earn credit for life experiences **#805**
- Find two-for-one tuition deals **#813**
- Get tuition discounts with an alumni referral **#816**
- Launch your own dorm room enterprise **#819**
- Locate the most lucrative internships and campus jobs **#861**
- Go to school part-time **#901**

And much, much more!

The Right Psychology

The great Green Bay Packers football coach Vince Lombardi once said, "The difference between a successful person and others is not a lack of strength, not a lack of knowledge, but rather a lack of will."

We can arm you with all of the resources and knowledge that you need to pay for college. But we cannot provide you with the motivation to make it happen. Few people talk about the psychology that you need to pay for college. In interviewing thousands of students, we have noticed that along with the knowledge there is also a mental aspect. Paying for college is not easy but neither is anything else that is worth having. So to stay in the game you need to have the right frame of mind. Here are the characteristics that we found to be shared by the students who were able to successfully find ways to pay for college even though they had little or no money of their own:

Persistence. This is a key trait. You need to continue despite any setbacks that you may face. We applied to many scholarships that we didn't win, but we never let that prevent us from applying to the next one.

Creativity. Some of the most successful students we met adapted methods to pay for college to their own situation. In this book you'll learn all of the ways that you can pay for college. However, for your specific case you may need to be creative about how you apply a specific example to yourself.

Long-term vision. The struggle to pay for school is a marathon, not a sprint. It involves adding up little victories here and there throughout the time you are in college. Break down your challenge into smaller pieces, and take it one step at a time. Just like putting money in the bank, to reach your goal you need to start with one penny and then add another and another.

Faith. You need a little faith to play this game. This is not the lottery, and there are no immediate results. Filling out the FAFSA form to apply for financial aid is a lot of work, and the outcome is far from guaranteed. Have faith that what you are doing will pay off in the long run.

Just as we did, in your quest for money for college you'll have your fair share of successes and failures. Having the right mindset is what propels you forward toward your goal. Keep these psychological pointers in mind as you read through this book and especially when you start to put these ideas into action.

Whether you just need a few extra dollars or to foot

your entire tuition bill, we're confident that the ideas that follow will inspire you to find ways to pay for your education. Your education is the most important investment that you'll make in yourself. It will set you up for a lifetime of success. Now let's look at the many ways that you can make this investment affordable.

CHAPTER
TWO

Win A Scholarship

How To Find A Scholarship

The best money is free money, and there is no better free cash for college than scholarships. We personally used scholarships to pay for a significant part of our education. We started during our junior year in high school and didn't stop until we had graduated from college. In total, we won over $100,000 in scholarships. While this may seem like a lot we've met students who have won much more.

One student we know won over $2 million in scholarships. Of course, she couldn't use all of this money since it was more than the entire cost of her college. But what a problem to have! Too much free money! Another student we met was a senior in high school when he started applying for scholarships. By graduation he had applied to 95 scholarships. Of these he only won seven. However, these seven totaled more than $48,000. Not too shabby for only one year of work. And he can't wait to continue applying for scholarships once in college!

There are two important steps to finding a scholarship:

Step 1: Become an expert on what scholarships are available. How can you find something if you don't know what you're looking for? That's the situation many students find themselves in when starting their scholarship search. For example, did you know that many unions give scholarships to the children of members? If you didn't then you probably would never even think to ask your parents if they are members of a union. Or how about this one: Did you know that professional sports teams award scholarships that have nothing to do with athletics? If you didn't then you might have totally ignored looking for scholarships from your hometown major league baseball team.

The best way to learn what scholarships are available is to expose yourself to as many scholarships as possible—even if they are not ones you will apply to win. By doing this you will get a better idea of what is out there and it will jumpstart your thinking about where to look. We recommend that besides

Finding the right scholarship is like ... looking for the perfect pair of pants

Here's an analogy to help you see why choosing the right scholarships is critical to actually winning a scholarship. Imagine that you are looking for the perfect pair of jeans at an outlet store. If you run in and grab the first pair on the rack, chances are it won't fit. It will probably pinch or sag in all the wrong places. But if take spend your time to dig through the piles of clothes, search out the racks in the back of the store and try everything on before you buy you'll leave with the perfect pair.

Finding a scholarship is no different. You need to know where to look and give yourself enough time to pick and choose from what you find. If you make sure that a scholarship fits your unique background, talents or achievements, you insure that you don't waste your time on scholarships you won't win. Just like pants, make sure the scholarship fits before you apply.

reading this chapter you also pick up a good scholarship directory such as our book, *The Ultimate Scholarship Book*, and start flipping through the pages. Even though there will be awards that you won't be eligible for, by exposing yourself to what is available you will start to make connections between your background, interests and future goals and various sources for free money.

Step 2: Search everywhere for scholarships that fit you. Too many students begin and end their scholarship search on the Internet. Then, after finding a bunch of awards they blindly fire off applications. What a terrible way to try to win. It will only result in a pile of rejection letters and even more frustration.

To maximize your chances of winning a scholarship you need to look everywhere—and that means getting out of your chair and looking beyond the Internet. Some of the best scholarships are found far from the beaten path. It takes more time and effort to find these scholarships but if you are willing to do some detective work you will be rewarded with a ton of scholarship opportunities.

The Golden Rule Of Searching For Scholarships

In this chapter we'll show you all of the places where you can find scholarships. As you start your own search, you'll undoubtedly turn up all kinds of awards—probably more than you'll ever have time to apply to. But don't stop looking. If there is one golden rule for finding a scholarship it is to never stop looking. You simply never know where you might discover the perfect award.

I (Kelly) actually found a scholarship as the result of having a headache. I was taking a Tylenol and while looking at the little bottle noticed that Tylenol (http://www.tylenol.com/news/scholarship) offered a scholarship. That headache turned out to be worth $1,500. It was the most lucrative headache I have ever had!

So put on your detective cap, and let's look at the best places to find scholarships. We will begin in a place that is just outside of your door: your own backyard.

Scholarship Gold Buried In Your Own Backyard

The most obvious place to find a scholarship is often the last place students look: in their own communities. While the prizes for backyard scholarships may not be as large as the more widely publicized national awards, they often have significantly less competition. This means you are much more likely to win. Think about it. Would you rather lose a $10,000 nationwide scholarship competition or win a $1,000 scholarship from your community?

Winning several backyard scholarships adds up quickly. Our own experience is proof. When we tell people that we won over $100,000 in awards, they oftentimes assume that we won one or two jackpots. Nothing is farther from the truth. We were able to accumulate this money by winning lots of little scholarships, many from our own community. As long as the scholarship fits you should apply no matter how much (or little) it's worth.

With this in mind, let's explore your own backyard and see what kind of scholarship gold we can uncover.

1.

Avoid reinventing the wheel by visiting your counselor

We have never met a college or career counselor (and we have met thousands) who does not keep a list of local scholarships. Whether your counselor posts these scholarships on a bulletin board, lists them in a newsletter or updates them online, take the initiative to find out what they know. Whenever a new scholarship is created the organization will usually send a notice to counselors at nearby schools. Over the years counselors become familiar with dozens of local awards. Most can tell you what scholarships are offered by the clubs and organizations in your community. They can give you leads on tracking down scholarships offered by local businesses and even awards sponsored by alumni. Take advantage of the knowledge your counselors already have. It will save you valuable time that you can spend applying to more scholarships.

2.

Service clubs are there to serve you

Remember that breakfast sponsored by the Lions Club that your parents dragged you to on Saturday morning? Ever wonder why these community clubs have such fundraisers? It's to help students like you, silly! Service organizations like the Lions Club (as well as dozens of others) raise money to provide scholarships to students in their communities. Look online and make a list of the service clubs in your community. While you're at it, why not dial the number and ask if they offer a scholarship?

Keep in mind that most service clubs also belong to a national organization. Both the local and the national organization may offer their own scholarships. The Kiwanis International Foundation offers scholarships for Key Club members as well as oratorical and talent contests.

In addition to looking online, visit your community center. The people who work there should know the names of most of the service clubs in your community. Your local public librarian can also help you find these organizations. To get you started here are a few of the most common service clubs. The websites provided are for the national organization. On the national website you can not only find out if they offer a scholarship but also find the contact information of local chapters.

While the following service organizations may offer awards at the national level, some only offer scholarships through their local chapters. If you don't find information about awards through the national organization, you can still use their website to locate your local chapter.

3. Altrusa
http://www.altrusa.com
This international service organization proves that business is not all about the bottom line. Its members are business and professional leaders who are committed to community improvement through volunteerism. Your best bet is to contact your local chapter to see what scholarships are available.

4. American Legion and American Legion Auxiliary
http://www.legion.org and http://www.legion-aux.org
This community service organization has almost 3 million members who are all veterans. Almost every city and town in

---

What is the purpose of the scholarship essay?

There are two main reasons that you are asked to submit an essay with your scholarship application.

The first is to show the scholarship judges why you deserve to win the scholarship. This does not mean that you should overtly campaign for your victory, composing a top 10 list of why you should be the winner, but you want to point out your achievements and be proud of your accomplishments.

The second reason why you are asked to write an essay is to share something about yourself that is not conveyed in your application. Scholarship committees view essays as a way to learn more about you and to gain insight into who you really are. Don't just list off accomplishments that are also found in your application. Use your essay to help the scholarship judges get to know you better.

America has an American Legion post. With such a membership, you might expect that you'd need some connection to the military to win a scholarship. In truth what is most important is that you can demonstrate your contribution to your community. Military service is not required. Both the American Legion and its sister organization, the American Legion Auxiliary, place a high value on community service that is reflected in their scholarships. On the national level ask about the *Eagle Scout Award, Oratorical Contest, Nursing Scholarship, Girl Scout Achievement Award, National President Scholarship, Samsung Scholarship, Non-Traditional Student Scholarship* and *Spirit of Youth Scholarship.*

5. The American Red Cross
http://www.redcross.org
Through its many local chapters the Red Cross provides a variety of services particularly during times of national disasters. The Red Cross also sponsors the Junior Red Cross. If you have volunteered with the organization, ask about the *Navin Narayan Scholarship.*

6. The Association of Junior Leagues International
http://www.ajli.org
This women's organization is committed to promoting volunteerism, developing the potential of women and improving communities. Contact your local chapter to see what scholarships may be available.

7. Boys and Girls Clubs
http://www.bgca.org
Each club provides programs that promote and enhance the development of children as well as give them a safe place to go after school. Most of their scholarships are club-based, which means you need to find and apply through your local club.

8. Campus Outreach Community League (COOL)
http://www.cool2serve.org
Student activists, volunteers and community leaders are all welcome to become members of this club. This non-profit group seeks to mobilize college students to get involved with their communities by supporting campus-based community service programs. Check with your campus COOL club to see what scholarship opportunities may be available.

9. Circle K

http://www.circlek.org

This is the college version of Kiwanis International and is dedicated to helping students become responsible leaders and citizens. On the national level ask about the *Past International Presidents' Scholarship, Himmel Scholarship, J. Walker Field Endowed Scholarship* and the *Cunat Visionary Scholarship.*

10. Civitan

http://www.civitan.org

Counting Thomas Edison as one of its members, Civitan is a volunteer organization that serves individual and community needs with an emphasis on helping people with developmental disabilities. On the national level ask about the *Shropshire Scholarship.*

11. The Elks Club

http://www.elks.org

If you think that you are one of the top 500 high school students in the country, consider the *Most Valuable Student Scholarship* program from the Elks, which awards up to $15,000 per year. The Elks Club is a fraternal organization dedicated to charitable works and has more than 2,100 lodges and over 1.1 million members. On the national level ask about the *Most Valuable Student Scholarship, Eagle Scout Award, Emergency Educational Fund Grants, Gold Award* and *Legacy Awards.* Many lodges also give scholarships to students in the community.

12. Fraternal Order of Eagles

http://www.foe.com

Their slogan is "People Helping People." To make this a reality the Eagles build training centers around the world, raise money to combat heart disease and cancer and help those with disabilities and seniors. If you are a member ask about the *Eagles Memorial Fund.* Also, check your local club to see what scholarships they offer.

13. Friends of the Library

http://www.ala.org/united/

The Friends do a lot more than run the best used book fairs. They are instrumental in supporting and fundraising for your local public libraries. Both Friends of the Library as well as the your local library may offer community scholarships.

14. Kiwanis International
http://www.kiwanis.org
This is a worldwide club for service and community-minded individuals. Kiwanis perform all kinds of community-based service projects. You can get an early start in the organization in high school in the Key Club and an even earlier start in junior high school in the Builders Club. On the national level ask about the *Presidential Freedom Scholarships* and the *Kiwanis International Foundation Scholarships.* Be sure to also find your local club and inquire about their scholarship opportunities.

15. Knights of Columbus
http://www.kofc.org
The Knights of Columbus is the largest lay organization in the Catholic Church and supports a variety of community and charitable programs. While the local councils establish their own scholarships, on the national level the *Father Michael J. McGivney Vocations Scholarship* and the *Bishop Thomas V. Daily Vocations Scholarship* are available to help students who are in theology programs.

16. Lions Club International
http://www.lionsclubs.org
The International Association of Lions is the largest service organization in the world with more than 1.4 million members. Lions members are dedicated to community service and other charitable goals. Almost all scholarships are awarded by local chapters including the Leo Club, which is the youth version of the Lions Club. You don't have to be a Lions member to win.

17. The National Exchange Club
http://www.nationalexchangeclub.com
This all-volunteer service organization is committed to serving the community and igniting the spirit of community service throughout the country. The group is a strong advocate of youth programs and sponsors several recognition programs for students. On the national level ask about the *Youth of the Month Awards.*

18. The National Grange
http://www.nationalgrange.org
Members of this organization share a common interest in community involvement and agricultural and rural issues. Check with your state Grange association for specific scholarships.

19. NeighborWorks
http://www.nw.org
This group is dedicated to revitalizing neighborhoods through innovative local partnerships of residents, businesses and government. Contact your local NeighborWorks program to see if they offer a scholarship in your area.

20. Optimist International
http://www.optimist.org
If you're a strong writer or communicator, Optimist International offers several scholarships for you. Meeting the needs of young people in communities worldwide, Optimist International volunteers lead service projects to assist and empower youth. On the national level ask about the *International Communications Contest, International Essay Contest* and *International Oratorical Contest.*

21. Performing arts center
http://www.performingarts.net
You may think that your local performing arts center is just a place to watch singers and dancers. However, if you are a performer yourself, your local center may not only enhance you culturally but also financially. Often these non-profit organizations sponsor scholarship competitions in the arts.

22. Rotaract and Interact
http://www.rotaract.org
Affiliated with Rotary Clubs, Rotaract and Interact Clubs are aimed at students and young adults. The groups promote leadership and responsible citizenship, high ethical standards in business, international understanding and peace. On the local level inquire about the *District Scholarships.*

23. Rotary Club

http://www.rotary.org

If you dream of living or working abroad, the Rotary Club can help fulfill your dream through their *Ambassadorial Scholarship.* This club brings together business and professional leaders to provide humanitarian service, encourage high ethical standards and help build goodwill and peace in the world. On the national level ask about the *Ambassadorial Scholarships* and the *Cultural Ambassadorial Scholarships.* Many local clubs also sponsor scholarships in their communities.

24. Ruritan

http://www.ruritan.org

Don't think that you will miss out on scholarships just because you don't live in a major metropolitan area. Ruritan, a civic organization made up of local clubs in small towns and rural communities, offers several awards for students. Ask your local club about the *Student Scholarship Program* and if they participate in the *Double Your Dollar Educational Grant Program.*

25. Salvation Army

http://www.salvationarmyusa.org

The Salvation Army is dedicated to caring for the poor and feeding the hungry. It also sponsors and supports many youth programs. Check your local organization to see if they offer college scholarships.

26. Sertoma International

http://www.sertoma.org

Their name stands for "SERvice TO MAnkind." This volunteer organization is dedicated to helping people with speech, hearing and language disorders. On the national level ask about the *Hearing Impaired Scholarships* and the *Communicative Disorders Scholarship Program.*

27. Soroptimist International of the Americas (SIA)

http://www.soroptimist.org

Your efforts may be rewarded with a scholarship if you're a young woman who volunteers, especially if your work benefits girls or women. Soroptimist members include women of all professions who believe in the importance of awareness, advocacy and action in the service of community and society. On the national level ask about the *Violet Richardson Award* and the *Woman's Opportunity Awards Program.*

28. U.S. Jaycees
http://www.usjaycees.org
The U.S. Junior Chamber (Jaycees) provides its members with an opportunity to develop as leaders in their communities by getting involved with civic affairs. On the national level ask about the *War Memorial Fund Scholarship, Thomas Wood Baldridge Scholarship* and *Charles R. Ford Scholarship.* Membership is not required for many of the awards.

29. Veterans of Foreign Wars (VFW)
http://www.vfw.org
This advocacy group for veterans is also committed to promoting volunteerism and community service. The VFW and its Ladies Auxiliary sponsor on the national level the *Voice of Democracy Audio Essay Contest, Patriot's Pen Youth Essay Contest, Teacher of the Year Award, Outstanding Scouts Award* and the *Hero's Recognition Program.* Don't forget to check with your local VFW post to find any specific scholarships aimed at students in your community.

30. White House Office of Social Innovation and Civic Participation
http://www.whitehouse.gov/administration/eop/sicp
This national effort to encourage volunteerism is coordinated at the White House. Its mission is to strengthen our culture of service and help find opportunities for every American to volunteer. Look at the prizes and challenges under the office's initiatives.

31. YMCA/YWCA
http://www.ymca.net
When you think of the YMCA, you might envision summer camp. But what you should think of is scholarships. With more than 2,400 branches this organization provides a host of health and social services to the community. Contact your local Y to find out about scholarship opportunities.

**When should I start applying for scholarships?
When is it too late to apply for scholarships?**

Our mantra is simple: It's never too early or too late to apply for scholarships. If you can believe it, there are scholarships that you can win as early as seventh grade!

On the other hand, you also don't want to stop applying for scholarships just because you graduated from high school. You can continue to apply for scholarships throughout your time in college or graduate school.

32. Zonta International
http://www.zonta.org
This organization of business executives and professionals is dedicated to the improvement of the status of women worldwide. On the national level ask about the *Amelia Earhart Fellowship Fund, Jane M. Klausman Women in Business Scholarship Fund* and the *Young Women in Public Affairs Fund.*

33.

Scholarships from religious organizations
If you are a member of an organized religion ask your minister, pastor, reverend, rabbi, priest or monk if the church sponsors a scholarship. Many religious organizations offer awards to members of their congregation. If they don't, politely suggest that they should.

Make sure you also check out the national or international organization of the church. In addition to any scholarships that the local church awards, the national office of the Presbyterian Church, for example, also awards scholarships nationally. Below is just a sample of the organized religions that offer scholarships to their members.

34. Assemblies of God
http://www.ag.org
On the national level the church offers a variety of scholarships including the *National Youth Scholarship* and the *Touch With Hope*

Scholarship for single mothers. The website also has a special section on college planning for Assemblies of God members at http://colleges.ag.org.

35. Baptist Church
http://www.abc-usa.org
The American Baptist Churches support American Baptist undergraduate, graduate and seminary students. To support growth in ministry skills, the church also assists pastors and those in other church vocations. All applicants must be members of an American Baptist church for at least one year before applying.

36. Catholic Church
https://www.catholicunitedfinancial.org
Catholic United Financial provides educational support through the *College Tuition Scholarship*. If you are a member of the First Catholic Slovak Ladies Association (http://www.catholicworkman.org) you may also qualify for their scholarship program.

37. Church of Jesus Christ of Latter-Day Saints
http://www.byu.edu
If you plan to attend Brigham Young University, check out the website and visit the department in which you plan to major. Most have a list of scholarships available to students within the major and some are designated for Mormons.

38. Evangelical Lutheran Church
http://www.elca.org
Begin your search at the website of the Evangelical Lutheran Church in America. You can search the site for specific scholarships as well as find links to related organizations such as the Women of the Evangelical Lutheran Church in America. This group in particular offers a number of scholarships including the *Opportunity Scholarships for Lutheran Laywomen*.

39. Judaism
http://www.hillel.org
There are a variety of scholarships for Jewish students. A good starting point is the Hillel, which sponsors several grant and scholarship competitions as well as produces several useful

guides for Jewish students. Another useful resource is the Bureau of Jewish Education, which has branches in most major cities. You can use the telephone book or a search engine like Google or Yahoo to find the one nearest you. Once you locate your bureau you'll find that it often has a list of scholarships for local Jewish students. The website for the bureau in San Francisco (http://www.jewishlearningworks.org), for example, has a page that lists most of the scholarships for Jewish students in Northern California.

40. Methodist Church
http://www.umc.org
The church sponsors several scholarship programs including the *Foundation Scholarship Program*, which awards $1,000 scholarships to more than 400 students. The church also has *Ethnic Minority Scholarships* and *General Scholarships* for older students and students who demonstrate leadership. The General Commission on Archives and History (http://www.gcah.org) also offers several research and writing grants for students interested in studying the history of the church.

41. Presbyterian Church
http://www.pcusa.org
The church offers a variety of awards to members who are enrolled in college. High school seniors can apply for the *National Presbyterian College Scholarship*, graduate students can apply for the *Continuing Education Grant* and medical students can apply for the *Grant Program for Medical Studies*.

42. Seventh-Day Adventist
http://www.adventist.org
Visit the church's website to find scholarship programs sponsored by individual churches. On the national level there is also the *General Conference Women's Ministries Scholarship Program* (http://wm.gc.adventist.org), which has awarded more than 550 scholarships since 1994. The scholarships are for women who plan to attend a Seventh-Day Adventist college and who otherwise would be unable to afford a Christian education.

43. Society of Friends (Quakers)
http://www.fum.org

The United Society of Friends Women International administers the *John Sarrin Scholarship*. This award provides money for students preparing for ministry.

44. United Church of Christ

http://www.ucc.org

The church offers the *UCC Seminarian Scholarship* for students preparing for ministry. Certain colleges have also designated funds for students who are members of the United Church of Christ. Currently the colleges with special scholarships for UCC students include Catawba College, Cedar Crest College, Dillard University, Doane College, Drury University, Elmhurst College, Elon College, Heidelberg College, Hood College, Lakeland College, Olivet College, Pacific University, Ripon College and Talladega College. You can check the national website for any additions to this list. In addition, the national offices of the United Church of Christ offer a limited number of awards from individual donors.

45.

Money from your parents' worker's union

If your parents or even grandparents belong to a union or if you plan to enter a field that has a union, check the union for scholarships. The Teamsters, for example, offer the *James R. Hoffa Memorial Scholarship Fund* for the children of its members. The union gives 75 scholarships a year of $1,000 to $10,000 per award. You can learn more at http://www.teamster.org.

For some scholarships, you must have a family member who is a member of the organization. For others, you don't have to be a member but must plan to enter a related career field. Contact the unions through either the address listed below or their website. Even better, have Mom or Dad ask their union directly. The following list of unions offer scholarship programs for their members, for the children of their members or for students entering related career fields.

46. Air Line Pilots Association

Undergraduate College Scholarship
1625 Massachusetts Avenue, NW, Suite 800

Washington, DC 20036
http://www.alpa.org

47. American Federation of School Administrators
AFSA Scholarship Awards
1101 17th Street, NW, Suite 408
Washington, DC 20036
https://www.facebook.com/AFSAUnion/

48. American Federation of State, County and Municipal Employees
AFSCME Family Scholarship
1625 L Street, NW
Washington, DC 20036
http://www.afscme.org

49. American Federation of Teachers
Robert G. Porter Scholars Program
555 New Jersey Avenue, NW
Washington, DC 20001
http://www.aft.org

50. American Federation of Television and Radio Artists
Scholarships of the AFTRA Heller Memorial Foundation
5757 Wilshire Boulevard, 7th Floor
Los Angeles, CA 90036
http://www.sagaftra.org

51. Association of Flight Attendants-CWA
Association of Flight Attendants Annual Scholarship
501 Third Street NW
Washington, DC 20001
http://www.afacwa.org

52. Bakery, Confectionery, Tobacco Workers and Grain Millers International Union
BCTGM Scholarship and *Vaughn Ball Memorial Scholarship*
10401 Connecticut Avenue, Floor 4
Kensington, MD 20895
http://www.bctgm.org

How do I write a winning scholarship essay?

When it comes to winning a scholarship you often need to write a powerful essay. Your essay is critical to convincing the judges to give you their money. When you are writing your scholarship essay, don't make any of the following mistakes:

Missing the question. It seems obvious, but enough students make this mistake that it needs to be emphasized: Be sure your essay answers the question.

Not having a point. If you cannot summarize the point of your essay in a single sentence, you may not have one.

Topic is too broad. Don't try to cover too much in the limited space of the essay.

Mechanical errors. Spelling and grammatical errors signal carelessness.

Not revealing something about you. Regardless of what the essay is about, it needs to reveal something about who you are, what motivates you or what is important to you.

Being ordinary. For your essay to stand out from the pile of other applicants, either the topic needs to be unique or the approach original.

If you want to learn more about writing a winning essay as well as read examples of 30 successful scholarship essays, take a look at our book, *How to Write a Winning Scholarship Essay.*

53. Boilermakers, Iron Ship Builders, Blacksmiths, Forgers and Helpers (IBB)
IBB Scholarship Program
753 State Avenue, Suite 570
Kansas City, KS 66101
http://www.boilermakers.org

54. Bricklayers and Allied Craftworkers (BAC)
Harry C. Bates Merit Scholarship
620 F Street, NW

Washington, DC 20004
http://www.bacweb.org

55. Brotherhood of Locomotive Engineers and Trainmen
International Western Convention (IWC) and *GIA Scholarship*
7061 East Pleasant Valley Road
Independence, OH 44131
http://www.ble.org

56. Chemical Workers Union Council, (UFCW)
Walter L. Mitchell Memorial Scholarship
1655 West Market Street, 6th Floor
Akron, OH 44313
http://www.icwuc.net

57. Communications Workers of America
CWA Joe Beirne Foundation Scholarship
501 Third Street, NW
Washington, DC 20001
http://www.cwa-union.org

58. Glass, Molders, Pottery, Plastics and Allied Workers International Union
Memorial Scholarship
60 Boulevard of the Allies
Pittsburgh, PA 15222
https://www.usw.org/union/mission/industries/glass

59. Graphic Communications International Union
Anthony J. DeAndrade Scholarship
25 Louisiana Avenue, NW
Washington, DC 20001
http://www.teamster.org/divisions/graphic-communications

60. International Alliance of Theatrical Stage Employees, Artists and Allied Crafts of the U.S.
Richard F. Walsh Award, Alfred W. DiTolla Award and *Harold P. Spivak Foundation Award*
207 W. 25th Street, 4th Floor
New York, NY 10001
http://www.iatse.net

61. International Association of Heat and Frost Insulators and Allied Workers
International Association of Heat and Frost Insulators and Allied Workers Scholarship
9602 M.L. King Jr. Highway
Lanham, MD 20706
http://www.insulators.org

62. International Association of Machinists and Aerospace Workers
International Association of Machinists and Aerospace Workers Scholarship for Members and *International Association of Machinists and Aerospace Workers Scholarship for Members' Children*
9000 Machinists Place, Room 204
Upper Marlboro, MD 20772
http://www.goiam.org

63. International Organization of Masters, Mates and Pilots
International Organization of Masters, Mates and Pilots Scholarship
700 Maritime Boulevard, Suite B
Linthicum Heights, MD 21090
http://www.bridgedeck.org

64. International Union of Electronic, Electrical, Salaried, Machine and Furniture Workers-Communications Workers of America (IUE-CWA)
The IUE-CWA International Paul Jennings Scholarship
2701 Dryden Road
Dayton, OH 45439
http://www.iue-cwa.org

65. International Union of Painters and Allied Trades of the United States and Canada
S. Frank Bud Raftery Scholarship
7234 Parkway Drive
Hanover, MD 21076
http://www.iupat.org

66. Iron Workers, International Association of Bridge, Structural, Ornamental and Reinforcing
John H. Lyons, Sr., Scholarship Program
1750 New York Avenue, NW, Suite 400
Washington, DC 20006
http://www.ironworkers.org

67. National Alliance of Postal and Federal Employees
Ashby B. Carter Memorial Scholarship
1640 11th Street, NW
Washington, DC 20001
http://www.napfe.com

68. National Association of Letter Carriers
Ashby B. Carter Memorial Scholarship
100 Indiana Avenue, NW
Washington, DC 20001
http://www.nalc.org

69. Office and Professional Employees International Union
Howard Coughlin Memorial Scholarship and *John Kelly Labor Studies Scholarship*
80 Eighth Avenue, 20th Floor
New York, NY 10011
http://www.opeiu.org

70. Professional and Technical Engineers, International Federation
Professional and Technical Engineers, International Federation Scholarship
501 3rd Street, NW, Suite 701
Washington, DC 20001
http://www.ifpte.org

71. Retail, Wholesale and Department Store Union District Council (RWDSU)
Alvin E. Heaps Memorial Scholarship
370 Seventh Avenue, Suite 501
New York, NY 10001
http://www.rwdsu.info

Is it worth it to apply for a scholarship even though I'm not guaranteed to win?

In our case it certainly was. We earned more money per hour applying for scholarships than we could have at any part-time job. But was our experience unique?

When we wrote *How to Write a Winning Scholarship Essay*, we interviewed hundreds of students who won scholarships. We selected 30 to feature in the book and asked them to estimate how many hours they spent in total applying for scholarships. This includes searching for awards and completing the applications—both for awards they won and lost. Then we took the total amount of money that they won and divided it into the total hours.

The result was that on average these students were making $300 per hour from their scholarship efforts. Now if you can find a part-time job that pays more than $300 an hour then take the job and forget about scholarships. If you can't, then we strongly recommend that you consider applying.

Sure there is no guarantee that you will win every scholarship. We certainly lost more than we won. But of the scholarships that you do win, you will find that the amount will more than make up for all of your hard work and time.

72. Screen Actors Guild
John L. Dales Scholarship
5757 Wilshire Boulevard, 7th Floor
Los Angeles, CA 90036
http://www.sagaftra.org

73. Seafarers International Union of North America
Charlie Logan Scholarship Program for Dependents
5201 Auth Way
Camp Springs, MD 20746
http://www.seafarers.org

74. Service Employees International Union
SEIU-Jesse Jackson Scholarship, Service Employees International Union

Scholarship and *Union Women Summer School Scholarship*
c/o Scholarship Program Administrators Inc.
1800 Massachusetts Avenue, NW
Washington, DC 20036
http://www.seiu.org

75. Sheet Metal Workers' International Association
Sheet Metal Workers' International Scholarship Fund
1750 New York Avenue, NW, 6th Floor
Washington, DC 20006
http://www.smart-union.org/sheet-metal/

76. Transport Workers Union of America
The Michael J. Quill Scholarship Fund
501 3rd Street, NW 9th Floor
Washington, DC 20001
http://www.twu.org

77. Union Plus
Union Plus Scholarship Program
1100 1st Street, NE Suite 850
Washington, DC 20002
http://www.unionplus.org

78. United Food and Commercial Workers Union
UFCW Suffridge Scholarship
1775 K Street, NW
Washington, DC 20006
http://www.ufcw.org

79. United Mine Workers of America
Lorin E. Kerr Scholarship Fund and *UMWA/BCOA Training and Education Fund*
18354 Quantico Gateway Drive, Suite 200
Triangle, VA 22172
http://www.umwa.org

80. United Transportation Union
United Transportation Union Scholarship
1750 New York Avenue NW, Sixth Floor

Washington, DC 20006
http://www.smart-union.org/td/

81. Utility Workers Union of America
Utility Workers Union of America Scholarship
1300 L Street, NW #1200
Washington, DC 20005
http://www.uwua.net

82.

Have your parents talk to their employer

Besides the annual company picnic, many employers offer scholarships as a benefit to employees. Have your parents check with their human resources (HR) department or manager to see if their company offers a scholarship program.

The children of Wal-Mart employees, for example, are eligible to compete for the *Walton Family Foundation Scholarship*, which is worth $8,000. Wal-Mart gives out 120 of these scholarships per year. Find out more at http://foundation.walmart.com.

You may be surprised to find that your parents' employers, whether international conglomerates or local businesses, offer awards.

83.

Win a scholarship for your parents' or grandparents' military service

If your parents or grandparents served in the U.S. Armed Forces you may qualify for a scholarship from a military association. Each branch of the service and even specific divisions within each branch have associations.

The 25th Infantry Division Association (http://www.25thida.com), for example, sponsors the *25th Infantry Division Association Scholarship* that aids the children and grandchildren of active and former members. The American Legion Auxiliary (http://www.legion-aux.org) offers the *National President Scholarship* for children of veterans. Speak with your parents and grandparents about their military service and ask if they belong to or know of any of the military associations. Also, see Chapter 14 for more military awards.

84.

Hit up your employer

Flipping burgers may have an upside. Even if you work only part-time you may qualify for an educational scholarship given by your employer. Speaking of burgers, McDonald's offers the *National Employee Scholarship* to reward the accomplishments of its student-employees. Every year, McDonald's selects one outstanding student-employee from each state to receive a $1,000 scholarship. In addition, the employee who demonstrates the highest commitment to school, work and community service is named *McScholar of the Year* and receives a $5,000 scholarship. Now that is something to flip for! Get more details at http://www.mcdonalds.com/usa/good/community.html. So, if you have a full- or part-time job, be sure to ask your employer about a scholarship.

85.

Get cash from your hometown professional sports team

Is your city the home of a professional sports team? If so contact the front office to see if they offer scholarships. In our area the Major League Baseball team the San Francisco Giants sponsors the *Junior Giants Scholarship*. Each year the Giants select 10 eighth grade scholars to receive a $2,500 scholarship if they successfully complete high school and go to college. Visit the Giants' website at http://sanfrancisco.giants.mlb.com and click on the "community" link.

Visit the official website of your hometown professional teams (see the addressed listed below) and look for a "community," "foundation" or "player's foundation" link. If you don't find information about scholarships, contact the team directly since sometimes their awards are not well publicized on their websites.

86. Major League Baseball
http://www.mlb.com

87. National Basketball Association
http://www.nba.com

88. National Football League
http://www.nfl.com

89. National Hockey League
http://www.nhl.com

90. Professional Golf Association Foundation
http://www.pgafoundation.com

91. Women's National Basketball Association
http://www.wnba.com

92.

Don't ignore businesses big and small

As a way to say "thank you" to customers, many businesses offer scholarships for students who live in their community. If your city is the home of a large company then you can almost bet that they offer a scholarship.

As an example, the Bill and Melinda Gates Foundation (http://www.gatesfoundation.org) offers scholarships for students who attend selected schools in the state of Washington, where Microsoft is based.

To find businesses in your area, check with your local chamber of commerce. You can visit the national chamber of commerce online at http://www.uschamber.com and from there you can find your local chamber. Most chambers maintain a directory of member companies that you can view.

While you are searching don't ignore the more successful mom and pop businesses either. In communities across America countless grocery stores, restaurants and even pet shops fund scholarships for students in their areas.

93.

Scholarships from your extracurricular activities

Besides doing what you enjoy, an added benefit of being involved in an extracurricular activity is that you may qualify for a scholarship. Ask your activity advisor if your group offers a scholarship for members. Also, if your club is part of a national organization, check with the national office to see if they sponsor a scholarship. The National Honor Society (https://www.nhs.us), for example, gives scholarships through both the local school chapters and through the national organization. Some scholarships offered by the national organization may require nomination by your local club. Don't let that stop you. Just ask your advisor to nominate you!

The following are some of the more popular extracurricular activities that have national affiliations. Remember to check with both your local and national parent chapter.

94. American Mensa Society
http://www.us.mensa.org

95. Amnesty International
http://www.amnesty.org

96. BETA Club
http://www.betaclub.org

97. Boy Scouts
http://www.scouting.org

98. Boys and Girls Club of America
http://www.bgca.org

99. DECA
http://www.deca.org

100. Educational Theatre Association
http://www.edta.org

101. Enactus
http://enactus.org

102. Family, Career and Community Leaders of America
http://www.fhahero.org

103. 4-H Clubs
http://www.fourhcouncil.edu

104. Fraternity or sorority
Contact your national chapter to learn what awards may be available to members.

105. Future Business Leaders of America
http://www.fbla-pbl.org

106. Future Farmers of America
http://www.ffa.org

107. Girl Scouts
http://www.girlscouts.org

108. Interact Club
http://www.rotary.org

109. Junior Achievement
http://www.ja.org

110. Key Club
http://www.keyclub.org

111. Leo Club
http://www.lionsclubs.org

112. Model United Nations
http://www.nmun.org

113. Mu Alpha Theta
http://www.mualphatheta.org

114. National Foundation for Teaching Entrepreneurship
http://www.nfte.com

115. The National Honor Society
https://www.nhs.us

116. National Rifle Association
http://www.nrahq.org

117. National Speech and Debate Association
https://www.speechanddebate.org

118. Quill and Scroll
http://www.quillandscroll.org

Are there weird scholarships like ones for left-handed students?

If you think that winning a scholarship based on your last name or your ability with duct tape is weird, well then the answer is yes, it is true that there are weird scholarships. These awards exist because wealthy alumni or donors with peculiar traits they want to promote make donations to colleges. Of course, the college is not going to turn down free money for its students. That's how many of these strange scholarships are started. At the end of this chapter we highlight a few of the more off beat scholarships. As you search for scholarships you too will encounter some truly outrageous ones.

119. S.A.D.D.
http://www.saddonline.com

120. Skills USA
http://www.skillsusa.org

121.

Your college financial aid office is a gold mine

You might think of the financial aid office as only helping students with need-based financial aid. It's true that this is the first place that you should go if you have financial need. But even if you don't, this office can still be helpful. If you are already in college (or even if you just live near one) pay a visit to the financial aid office. This office serves as a clearinghouse for any scholarship opportunities at your school and within your community. Like high school counselors, many financial aid offices also maintain a list of scholarship opportunities. Even if you are not receiving financial aid you can still make an appointment to speak with a financial aid counselor about the various scholarship opportunities at your college.

122.

Career service offices offer more than job resources

When you are a college senior and looking for a job, the career service office will become your second home. However, many career service offices also keep lists of scholarships and in particular those that might help you get a summer internship or even pay for you to study abroad. Don't wait until your last year in college to see what the career service office has to offer.

123.

Visit your department's administrative assistant

One of the most valuable people at your college is not the president or the dean or even your favorite professor, it's the administrative assistant of your department. This one person knows more about what happens in your major than any other person. They have probably been in the department the longest. Take some time to talk to the department administrative assistant. Ask him or her about what kind of scholarship opportunities and competitions are available to students with your major.

When I (Gen) was a history major at Harvard I asked the department assistant what kind of scholarships were available. She reached under her desk and pulled out a thick binder filled with scholarships. "You are the first person to ask to see the binder this year," she said as she handed it over. It was a gold mine of scholarships and all I had to do was ask.

Here are just a few examples of what you might find. The University of Massachusetts at Amherst has such scholarships as the *Philip Weiss Memorial Scholarship* for students majoring in Judaic Studies, the *Butterworth Scholarship* for juniors and seniors studying floriculture or ornamental horticulture and the *Stephen R. Kellogg Scholarship* for sophomores in the civil and environmental engineering department. Just asking around within your own major will turn up a lot of possibilities.

124.

Take money from your local politicians for a change

Even if you didn't vote for them or if you aren't old enough to vote, you may get some help from your local politicians. Many establish scholarships for students who live in their district as way of saying "thank you" to their constituents. Contact your local politicians' offices to find out more.

125.

Search your community newspaper for past winners

Your local newspaper is a treasure map to finding local scholarships. In the fall and spring scholarship organizations announce their winners, and your community newspaper often prints their names. Go through back issues or search the newspaper articles online (search for the words "scholarship" and "scholarship winner") to find announcements of last year's winners. Note who gave the scholarship and find out if you can apply for the same award this year.

Flipping through our local newspaper recently we found an announcement of a student who won a scholarship sponsored by a group that promoted vegetarianism. If you are a vegetarian then you too may apply for this award at http://www.vrg.org. You just never know what you'll find in your community newspaper.

Searching Beyond Your Backyard

At some point you will exhaust your local resources. You will have knocked on the doors of the local businesses, pored through the back issues of the community newspaper and practically camped out in your financial aid office. When you get to this point, it's time to move on. We're talking about the big leagues–the national scholarships. There are scholarships from large businesses, professional associations and philanthropic and charitable organizations. There are awards based on academic interest, talent, future career goals, race and ethnicity and more. What ties all of these scholarships together is that they are open to students from across the country.

In general, scholarships offered outside your community give larger prizes. Unfortunately, they also attract more competition, but don't let that scare you. We have met hundreds of students who have won scholarships, and every single one who won a national level competition told us that they never expected it. Most even wondered beforehand if they should even spend the time to apply. If they had listened to their inner doubts they never would have won. It might sound trite, but it's true: You can't win if you don't apply.

Let's make the world our scholarship hunting ground and look for awards both far and wide.

126.

Unleash the power of the Internet

The Internet puts the world's biggest library at your fingertips and allows you access to an unprecedented amount of information. It can also be truly frustrating. The problem with searching for scholarships online is that there is no filtering. Type in the word "scholarship" into a search engine and you'll get over 100,000 results. Only a tiny fraction of these results will actually be useful to you. To solve this problem of too much information there are specialized websites that let you search databases of scholarships. For the best of these, you fill out some information about yourself and with the click of a mouse are matched to scholarships that you can apply to win.

Sound too easy? In some ways it is. Don't rely on these websites to find every scholarship that is right for you. Many students make the mistake of assuming that once they do a search they have exhausted all sources for scholarships. The reality is that no matter how many scholarships these websites claim to have in their database none of them even comes close to the total number of scholarships that are available. Don't rely on websites as your only means of finding scholarships. If you do you'll miss some of the best awards that can only be found through your own detective work.

Before we share our list of the best websites to search we want to warn you against using any website that charges you money to perform a search. There are enough good free websites that you should never have to pay for a scholarship search.

Now without further adieu, here are some of the better free websites that we recommend you search:

127. SuperCollege
http://www.supercollege.com

128. moolahSPOT
http://www.moolahspot.com

129. Sallie Mae
http://www.salliemae.com/scholarships

130. Scholarship Experts
http://www.scholarshipexperts.com

131. Zinch
http://www.zinch.com/scholarships

132. The College Board
http://www.collegeboard.com

133. Cornell University Mario Einaudi Center for International Studies
http://einaudi.cornell.edu/funding-opportunities/postdoc
This site is for international students, but many of the fellowships and scholarships listed are also open to non-international students.

134. The Princeton Review
http://www.review.com

135. CollegeXpress
http://www.collegexpress.com

136. Adventures In Education
http://www.aie.org

137. FastWeb
http://www.fastweb.com

138. Scholarships.com
http://www.scholarships.com

Does SuperCollege offer a scholarship?

Yes we do! Each year we use part of the proceeds from the sale of our books to award scholarships to outstanding high school and college students. This award is part of our ongoing mission to help you pay for the college of your dreams. So if you are a high school, college or graduate school student, visit our website to submit your application. There is no age limit, but you need to be a U.S. citizen or legal resident. You may study any major and attend or plan to attend any accredited college or university in the U.S. Visit our website to apply at http://www.supercollege.com.

139. Petersons
http://www.petersons.com

140. Student Scholarship Search
https://www.studentscholarshipsearch.com

141. CollegeNet
http://www.collegenet.com

142.

Hitting up big business

When you think about how many cars Toyota and Chevrolet sell or about how many Cokes the world consumes, you can see why large companies like these take some of their profits and return them to students like you through scholarships. These scholarship programs are often general in nature seeking students who are strong academically and in extracurricular activities, but some have a more specific aim. Tylenol, for example, offers scholarships for students entering health-related professions, which makes sense for a pharmaceutical company.

You have probably heard of many of the companies that offer scholarship programs simply because you buy their products. But one quick way to increase your knowledge of what businesses are out there is to read the business section of your newspaper. You can also find a list of big companies by looking at the Forbes Magazine website at http://www.forbes.com. Once you find some good prospects either email or call their human resources department and ask if they have a foundation or scholarship program. The following is just a sample of the more prominent "Big Business" scholarships. You'll notice that some of these awards don't even require that you have an interest in their industry.

143. AXA Achievement Scholarships
http://www.axa-equitable.com/axa-foundation/community-scholarships.html
Each branch of AXA awards up to twelve $2,000 scholarships to local high school seniors. Students must show "ambition and drive" and "determination to set and reach goals" among other traits.

144. Burger King Scholars Program
http://www.bkmclamorefoundation.org
The *Burger King Scholars Program* helps students who plan to enroll in a two- or four-year college or university, participate in community service and demonstrate financial need. Academic achievement and work experience are also considered.

145. Cargill Community Scholarship Program
http://www.cargill.com/about/citizenship/scholarships.htm
Cargill supports three scholarship programs that award more than $500,000 in scholarships annually. These scholarships are for students who live in and around Cargill communities as well as the children of employees.

146. Coca-Cola Scholars Program
http://www.coca-colascholars.org
The world drinks billions of Cokes each year and in return the company gives away almost $2 million in scholarships. Begun in 1986 to celebrate the Coca-Cola Centennial, the program is designed to contribute to the nation's future and to assist a wide range of students. Applicants must be high school seniors or community college students. Selection is based on character, leadership, academic achievement and motivation to serve and succeed.

147. Coca-Cola Two-Year College Scholarship
http://www.coca-colascholars.org
This program recognizes students enrolled in two-year programs for their academic achievement and community service. Applicants should be first- or second-year postsecondary students who intend to complete their education at a two-year degree school.

148. Commerce Bank Scholarship Sweepstakes
http://commercebank.secondstreetapp.com
Five awards are given each year to pay for college. Applicants must be 18 years or older and be enrolled at least part-time in a post-secondary educational institution.

149. Dell Scholars Program
http://www.msdf.org
Michael Dell is one of the most famous entrepreneurs to have started his computer business in his college dormroom. Now as a result of his company's success, through the Michael and Susan Dell Foundation, he awards scholarships to underprivileged high school seniors.

150. Dupont Challenge
http://thechallenge.dupont.com
This scholarship essay contest is open to students between grades 7 and 12. It is designed to help promote an interest in scientific studies.

151. Glamour's Top Ten College Women Competition
http://www.glamour.com
Who wouldn't want to be on the cover of Glamour? Not only could your face grace the October issue but you could also walk away with a $1,500 prize and a free trip to New York City. This competition is open to any woman who is a full-time college junior. Winners are selected based on leadership, involvement on campus and the community, academic excellence and future goals.

152. Hitachi Yoshiyama Award
http://www.hitachifoundation.org
The Yoshiyama Award recognizes exemplary service and com-

munity involvement. You must be nominated by a community leader, teacher, principal or clergy member.

153. Intel Science Talent Search
http://www.societyforscience.org/sts/
This is the granddaddy of all science fairs. This science competition is designed to recognize excellence in science among the nation's youth and encourage the exploration of science. A recent winner created a glove that can read sign language. First prize is a scholarship worth $100,000.

154. KFC Colonel's Scholars Program
http://www.kfcscholars.org
KFC provides more than chicken. The restaurant company gives scholarships of up to $20,000 to high school seniors who have entrepreneurial drive and financial need and who plan to attend an in-state public college or university.

155. Microsoft General Scholarships
http://www.microsoft.com/college/ss_overview.mspx
If you have ever used a computer, then you are probably familiar with Microsoft. The international software giant offers several scholarships for students, women and minorities. The scholarships are designed to reward students with a passion for software development and technology. Scholarships cover 100 percent of tuition.

156. Papa Johns Scholars
http://www.papajohns.com
Not at all based on your pizza-throwing ability, this program rewards high school seniors based on creativity, community involvement, academic achievement, quality of character, leadership, obstacles overcome, life goals and interests.

157. Prudential Spirit of Community Awards
http://www.prudential.com/community/spirit/
You need to be nominated by your middle or high school counselor or principal. Remember, you can always ask to be nominated. This award is based on community and volunteer activities.

158. Sam Walton Community Scholarship

http://foundation.walmart.com

The foundation of America's largest retailer rewards students who are active in their communities.

159. Siemens Competition in Math, Science and Technology

http://www.siemens-foundation.org

This science fair on steroids attracts high school students from across the country who are willing to challenge themselves through science research.

160. Toshiba Exploravision Awards

http://www.exploravision.org

Known for its own cutting-edge technology, Toshiba sponsors this competition for K-12 students that encourages combining imagination with the tools of science to create and explore a vision of a future technology.

161. Tylenol Scholarship

http://www.tylenol.com/news/scholarship

Paging future doctors and nurses. You can win one of ten $10,000 or one of 150 $1,000 scholarships from Tylenol if you are an undergraduate or graduate school student who has demonstrated leadership in community and school activities and who intends to enter a health-related field.

162.

Professional associations will pay you to go to school

Whether you want to be a computer scientist or certified fraud examiner there is a professional organization to support your profession. In fact, in the U.S. alone there are more than 135,000 professional associations. One of the missions of these organizations is to support students who want to enter the field by offering scholarships.

In our scholarship book, *The Ultimate Scholarship Book*, we list some of the best professional associations that offer scholarships. We also recommend that you check out the *Encyclopedia of Associations* published by the Gale Group. This multi-volume set is extremely expensive, but fortunately you can find this book at most college and state libraries.

Inside you will find a list of nearly every professional association in the U.S. Simply call or visit the websites of the associations that support your future career to see if they offer scholarships.

Another great way to track down professional associations is to talk to the people who are already in these careers. If you're a pre-med student, spend some time talking to doctors to learn which associations they belong to. You can also go to the library and read trade journals for the profession. Associations often advertise in these publications.

The following list is just a few examples of some professional associations that offer scholarships. Remember, there are more than 135,000 professional associations in existence!

163. Association of Certified Fraud Examiners
http://www.acfe.com
If you want to make a career out of detecting forged checks, you can apply for the *Ritchie-Jennings Memorial Scholarship,* which supports students who want to become Certified Fraud Examiners.

164. Academy of Motion Picture Arts and Sciences
http://www.oscars.org
An Oscar may be in your future, so get a head start on the golden guy with these scholarships. Future filmmakers and screenwriters can apply for the *Don and Gee Nicholl Fellowships in Screenwriting* and the *Student Academy Awards.*

165. Academy of Television Arts and Sciences Foundation
http://www.emmys.org
From the academy that presents the Emmys comes the *College Television Awards* for students who produce original films and videos.

166. Actors' Fund of America
http://www.aflcio.org
It may be hard to make ends meet working as a waiter while waiting for your big break. That's why the *Actors' Work Program* provides tuition and grants for job retraining for members of the entertainment industry.

167. Air Traffic Control Association

http://www.atca.org

If your dream is to someday direct the traffic in the sky, you should check out the *Air Traffic Control Association Scholarship Program.*

168. Aircraft Electronics Association

http://www.aea.net

This association offers a variety of awards for students interested in a career in avionics or aircraft repair. They administer the following awards: *Bendix/King Avionics Scholarship, Bud Glover Memorial Scholarship, David Arver Memorial Scholarship, Dutch and Ginger Arver Scholarship, Garmin Scholarship, Goodrich Aerospace Scholarship, Johnny Davis Memorial Scholarship, Lee Tarbox Memorial Scholarship, Lowell Gaylor Memorial Scholarship* and the *Mid-Continent Instrument Scholarship.*

169. American Angus Association

http://www.angus.org

Like Angus beef? Then you might want to apply for the *Angus Foundation Scholarship* for students who are active with the Angus breed.

170. American Association of Airport Executives

http://www.aaae.org

If you love airports and could think of nothing better than spending 40 hours a week working in one then check out the *AAAE Foundation Scholarship.*

171. American Association of Critical-Care Nurses

http://www.aacn.org

Active RN students and members of the AACN can apply for the *Educational Advancement Scholarship.*

172. American Bar Association

http://www.abanet.org/lsd/

Future lawyers can enter the *ABA Essay and Writing Competitions* or apply for the *Legal Opportunity Scholarship Fund.*

173. American Concrete Institute
http://www.aci-int.org
There is no construction industry without cement. If you are a college senior interested in entering the construction industry, you've got to check out the *Peter D. Courtois Concrete Construction Scholarship.*

174. American Criminal Justice Association
http://www.acjalae.org
Rewarding future crime fighters, the association offers both the *Scholarship Program* for undergraduate or graduate students who are studying criminal justice and a *Student Paper Competition* for student members.

175. American Culinary Federation
http://www.acfchefs.org
Future chefs take note. If you are in a culinary program take a look at these scholarships: the *Chain des Rotisseurs Scholarship,* the *Chair's Scholarship* and the *Ray and Gertrude Marshall Scholarship.*

176. American Dental Association
http://www.ada.org

What if the professional organization that gives the scholarship requires that I be a member to apply?

Most professional organizations do not require that you be a member to apply for a scholarship. However, if you find one that does and you are serious about the career (and you shouldn't really be applying if you're not), then why not join the association? Many offer discounted student memberships. Also, check with your department since some schools purchase group membership for all of their students. You get a lot out of joining an association so even if you have to pay the dues, it is usually well worth it.

If you want to pursue a career in dental hygiene, dental assisting, dentistry or dental laboratory technology take a look at the *Allied Dental Health Scholarship, Dental Student Scholarship* and the *Minority Dental Student Scholarship.*

177. American Institute of Chemical Engineers (AIChE)
http://www.aiche.org
If you're a member of an AIChE Student Chapter or Chemical Engineering Club you can apply for the *Donald F. and Mildred Topp Othmer Foundation Scholarship* or the *National Student Design Competition.* If you're not a member but are majoring in chemical engineering you can apply for the *John J. McKetta Scholarship.*

178. American Meteorological Society
http://www.ametsoc.org/AMS/
If you've ever dreamed of making it rain (or at least predicting when it will), look at these scholarships for atmospheric or oceanic studies: *AMS Undergraduate Scholarship, AMS Graduate Fellowship in the History of Science, Industry Minority Scholarship, Industry Undergraduate Scholarship, Industry/Government Scholarship* and the *Father James B. Macelwane Annual Awards in Meteorology.*

179. American Nuclear Society
http://www.ans.org
If you are a student in a nuclear-related field, check out the *ANS Graduate Scholarship*, the *ANS Undergraduate Scholarship* and the *John Muriel Landis Scholarship.*

180. American Nursery and Landscape Association
http://www.americanhort.org
If you have a green thumb then the *Timothy Bigelow and Palmer W. Bigelow, Jr. Scholarship* and *Usrey Family Scholarship* may be the perfect awards for you.

181. American Society of Agricultural and Biological Engineers
http://www.asabe.org
Biological or agricultural engineering majors are eligible for the *Adams Scholarship Grant*, the *ASAE Foundation Scholarship* and the *ASAE Student Engineer of the Year Scholarship.*

182. American Society of Ichthyologists and Herpetologists

http://www.asih.org

If you are a future ichthyologist or herpetologist check out the *Gaige Fund Award*, the *Raney Fund Award* and the *Stoye and Storer Award*.

183. American Society of Mechanical Engineers (ASME)

http://www.asme.org

ASME student members can apply to a number of scholarships including: the *ASME Foundation Scholarship*, the *F.W. Beichley Scholarship*, the *Frank and Dorothy Miller ASME Auxiliary Scholarship*, the *Garland Duncan Scholarship*, the *John and Elsa Gracik Scholarship*, the *Kenneth Andrew Roe Scholarship*, the *Melvin R. Green Scholarship* and the *Robert F. Sammataro Pressure Vessel Piping Division Scholarship*. (If you understand what this last scholarship is about you probably deserve to win it!)

184. American Society of Travel Agents Foundation

http://www.asta.org

We see travel in your future. If you do too then take a look at the various scholarship programs offered by this society, which include the *American Express Travel Scholarship*, the *Avis Scholarship*, the *Fernando R. Ayuso Award*, the *Healy Scholarship*, the *Holland America Line-Westours, Inc. Research Grant*, the *Joseph R. Stone Scholarship*, the *Princess Cruises and Princess Tours Scholarship*, the *Simmons Scholarship* and the *Southern California Chapter/Pleasant Hawaiian Holidays Scholarship*.

185. American Society of Women Accountants Scholarship

http://www.aswa.org

Attention number crunchers. If you are a female part-time or full-time student of accounting, contact your local ASWA chapter to receive an application for the *ASWA Scholarship*. You do not have to be a member to apply.

186. American Welding Society Foundation

http://www.aws.org

If you are living your dream of working in the spark-filled welding industry then you'll want to apply for the *James A. Turner, Jr. Memorial Scholarship*.

187. Armed Forces Communications and Electronics Association

http://www.afcea.org

First of all you don't have to be affiliated with the military to apply for these scholarships. However, they are geared toward students studying technical or scientific fields. Check out these awards: the *General John A. Wickham Scholarship, Ralph W. Shrader Scholarship* and the *Computer Graphic Design Scholarship.*

188. Associated General Contractors of America

http://www.agc.org

Planning on wearing a hard hat to work? If you are an undergraduate or graduate student in construction or civil engineering program you can apply for the *AGC Undergraduate* or *AGC Graduate Scholarship.*

189. Associated Male Choruses of America

http://amcofa.org

This association offers the *AMCA Music Scholarship* to promote chorus and music students in college.

190. Association for Women in Mathematics

http://www.awm-math.org

To support women who are studying mathematics this organization sponsors both the *Alice T. Schafer Prize* and the *AWM Biographies Contest.*

191. Association for Women in Science

http://www.awis.org

It's no secret that there are more men in the sciences than women. That's why the AWS sponsors the *Science Undergraduate Award* and the *Association for Women in Science Graduate Award* to encourage more women to get into the sciences.

192. Association of Food and Drug Officials

http://www.afdo.org

If your dream is to work for the FDA or if you are studying food, drug or consumer product safety you can apply for the *Association of Food and Drug Officials Scholarship Award.*

193. Association of State Dam Safety Officials
http://www.damsafety.org
Somebody has to keep the dam from bursting. If that person is you then don't ignore the *ASDSO Dam Safety Scholarship*.

194. Broadcast Education Association (BEA)
http://www.beaweb.org
This is the award for future Lester Holts and Katie Courics. If you are a college junior, senior or graduate student at a BEA member university you may be able to apply for the *Broadcast Education Association Scholarship*. The organization has members who are in the television and radio broadcasting industry as well as in telecommunications and electronic media.

195. Educational Foundation for Women in Accounting
http://www.efwa.org
Do you like working with numbers? If so, the *Women in Transition Scholarships* and *Women in Need Scholarships* both provide financial assistance to female students who are pursuing degrees in accounting. Trying to get a Ph.D. in accounting? You may be interested in the *Laurel Fund*.

196. Emergency Nurses Association
http://www.ena.org
To promote research and education in emergency care this association sponsors the *ENA Foundation Undergraduate Scholarship*, the *Karen O'Neil Endowed Advanced Nursing Practice Scholarship* and the *Medtronic Physio-Control Advanced Nursing Practice Scholarship*.

197. Entomological Society of America
http://www.entsoc.org
The *John Henry Comstock Graduate Student Award*, *Normand R. Dubois Memorial Scholarship* and *Stan Beck Fellowship* all support graduate and undergraduate students who are studying entomology.

198. Executive Women International (EWI)
http://www.ewiconnect.com
High school students can apply for the *Executive Women International Scholarship Program*. Single parents, individuals just

entering the workforce or displaced workers can all apply for an *Adult Students in Scholastic Transition* (ASIST) award.

199. Golf Course Superintendents Association of America Foundation

http://www.gcsaa.org

Do you always find yourself defending golf's place in the sporting kingdom? If the golfing industry is your passion you have your pick of scholarships for every aspect of the golf course industry including: the *GCSAA Footsteps on the Green Award*, the *GCSAA Scholars Program*, the *GCSAA Student Essay Contest* and the *Scotts Company Scholars Program*.

200. Herb Society of America

http://www.herbsociety.org

If you are passionate about studying herbs then you don't want to miss applying for an *HAS Research Grant*.

201. Industrial Designers Society of America

http://www.idsa.org

You may have the next winning design for robotic vacuum cleaners or 100 gigabyte mp3 players in you. Student industrial designers can apply for the *David H. Liu Memorial Graduate Scholarships in Product Design*, the *Gianninoto Graduate Scholarship* and the *IDSA Undergraduate Scholarship*.

202. International Association of Fire Fighters

http://www.iaff.org

Members of the IAFF can apply for the *Harvard University Trade Union Program Scholarship*. Selection is based on participation in your local IAFF affiliate.

203. International Food Service Executives Association

http://www.ifsea.org

You probably know that there is more to food services than food preparation. The industry needs students who are skilled in management. If you are studying a food service-related major then check out the *IFSEA Scholarship*.

204. The International Society for Optical Engineering

http://www.spie.org

This group offers the *Michael Kidger Memorial Scholarship* for students in the optical design field.

205. Iron and Steel Society

https://www.aist.org

To attract talented and dedicated students to careers within the iron and steel industries, this organization offers the *ISS Scholarship Foundation Scholarship.*

206. Karla Scherer Foundation Scholarship

http://karlascherer.org

Are you gunning to be a CFO of a major company? This award is for female students majoring only in finance or economics who plan to have corporate business careers.

207. National Association of Chiefs of Police

http://www.aphf.org

The *NACOP Scholarship* is for disabled officers who want to retrain through education. It is also open to the college-bound children of disabled officers.

208. National Association of Women in Construction

http://www.nawic.org

Don't think that only the guys get to have the fun with building things. If you are a female student enrolled in a construction-related degree program you can apply for the *Undergraduate Scholarship* and the *Construction Crafts Scholarship.*

209. National Community Pharmacists Association

http://www.ncpanet.org

Students who are enrolled in a college of pharmacy may apply for the $2,000 *NCPA Foundation Presidential Scholarship.*

210. National Press Photographers Foundation

http://www.nppa.org

If you are studying photojournalism or you want to enter this industry take at look at the following awards: the *Bob East*

How do I actually win a scholarship?

Winning a scholarship takes both time and effort. To help you increase your chances of winning observe these five "rules." If you want to learn more, take a look at our books, *Get Free Cash for College* and *How to Write a Winning Scholarship Essay*.

Be accurate and complete. More applications are disqualified because applicants didn't follow the directions than for any other reason.

Uncover the mission of the scholarship. Understand what the organization is trying to achieve by giving the scholarship and demonstrate how you match their goal in your application and essay.

Don't write your scholarship essay the night before. Give yourself time to write an essay that shows the judges exactly why you are the best candidate for their award by highlighting an experience or achievement that demonstrates how you match the goals of the scholarship.

Ace the interview. Interviews are often where final decisions are made, so be prepared by practicing your answers.

Don't be afraid to brag. This is not the time to be modest. Throughout your scholarship essay and interview explain why you deserve to win.

Scholarship, the *College Photographer of the Year Award*, the *Joseph Ehrenreich Scholarship*, the *Kit C. King Graduate Scholarship*, the *NPPF Still Photography Scholarship*, the *NPPF Television News Scholarship* and the *Reid Blackburn Scholarship*.

211. National Restaurant Association Educational Foundation

http://www.edfound.org

Students majoring in a food service- or restaurant-related program may apply for either the *Academic Scholarship for High School Seniors* or the *Academic Scholarship for Undergraduate College Students*.

212. National Scholastic Press Association
http://www.studentpress.org
Stop the presses! If you work on your high school newspaper you may apply for the *Wikoff Scholarship for Editorial Leadership.*

213. National Society of Accountants
http://www.nsacct.org
The *NSA Scholarship* is perfect for you if you're an undergraduate majoring in accounting with a minimum 3.0 GPA.

214. National Society of Professional Engineers
http://www.nspe.org
This association offers a variety of scholarships for future engineers including: the *NSPE Auxiliary Scholarship*, the *Paul H. Robbins, P.E., Honorary Scholarship*, the *Professional Engineers in Government Scholarship*, the *Professional Engineers in Industry Scholarship* and the *Virginia D. Henry Memorial Scholarship*.

215. National Speakers Association
http://www.nsaspeaker.org
Surveys show that people fear speaking in public more than death. The *Bill Gove Scholarship*, the *Cavett Robert Scholarship*, the *Nido Qubein Scholarship* and the *Earl Nightengale Scholarship* are for you if you don't feel that way.

216. National Student Nurses' Association
http://www.nsna.org
Students in a school of nursing or pre-nursing program may apply for the *National Student Nurses' Association Scholarship*.

217. Outdoor Writers Association of America
http://www.owaa.org
If writing, filming or creating art based on the great outdoors is what you love, you just might have a chance at the *Bodie McDowell Scholarship*.

218. Physician Assistant Foundation
http://www.aapa.org
AAPA members who attend an ARC-PA–accredited physician assistant program may apply for the *Physician Assistant Foundation Scholarship*.

219. Plumbing-Heating-Cooling Contractors National Association
http://www.phccweb.org
If you are currently in a p-h-c program (and if you are then you know this means plumbing-heating-cooling) you may be able to apply for either the *Delta Faucet Company Scholarship* or the *PHCC Educational Foundation Scholarship*.

220. Public Relations Student Society of America
http://www.prssa.org
Publicity hounds and members of the PRSSA may apply for the following scholarships: the *Gary Yoshimura Scholarship, Professor Sidney Gross Memorial Award,* the *Betsy Plank/PRSSA Scholarship* and the *Lawrence G. Foster Award for Excellence in Public Relations.*

221. Radio and Television News Directors Association
http://www.rtnda.org
If you plan to enter the fast-paced world of television or radio news broadcasting then you should investigate these awards: the *Abe Schechter Graduate Scholarship,* the *Carole Simpson Scholarship,* the *Ed Bradley Scholarship,* the *Ken Kashiwahara Scholarship,* the *Len Allen Award for Radio Newsroom Management,* the *Lou and Carole Prato Sports Reporting Scholarship,* the *Mike Reynolds Scholarship* and the *Undergraduate Scholarship.*

222. Society of American Registered Architects
https://www.sara-national.org
The group sponsors the *Student Design Competition* to help architecture students.

223. Society of Automotive Engineers
http://www.sae.org
Who knew that fixing up cars and trucks would lead you to a scholarship? This organization offers awards for high school, college and graduate students entering this industry including the *Doctoral Scholars Forgivable Loan Program,* the *Long-Term Member Sponsored Scholarship,* the *SAE Engineering Scholarship* and the *Yanmar/SAE Scholarship.*

224. Society of Exploration Geophysicists
http://students.seg.org
To encourage students who want to journey to the center of the earth (or at least pursue a career in exploration geophysics), this association offers the *SEG Scholarship.*

225. Society of Nuclear Medicine
http://www.snmmi.org
Students in nuclear medicine may apply for the *Paul Cole Scholarship Award.*

226. Society of Plastics Engineers
http://www.4spe.org
If you plan to enter the plastics industry then you are in luck. This organization offers a plethora of awards for future plastic people including the *American Plastics Council (APC)/SPE Plastics Environmental Division Scholarship,* the *Composites Division/Harold Giles Scholarship,* the *Polymer Modifiers and Additives Division Scholarship,* the *SPE General Scholarship,* the *Ted Neward Scholarship,* the *Thermoforming Division Memorial Scholarship,* the *Thermoset Division/James I. MacKenzie Memorial Scholarship* and (our favorite) the *Vinyl Plastics Division Scholarship.*

227. Society of Professional Journalists
http://www.spj.org
This group sponsors the *Mark of Excellence Awards* honoring the best in student journalism. There are awards in 45 categories for print, radio, television and online journalism.

228. SWE Society of Women Engineers
http://www.societyofwomenengineers.org
This organization offers *National SWE Scholarships* for students from freshmen in college through graduate and adult students.

229. University Aviation Association
http://www.uaa.aero
This group offers several awards for aviation students including the *Eugene S. Kropf Scholarship,* the *Gary Kiteley Executive Director Scholarship* and the *Joseph Frasca Excellence in Aviation Scholarship.*

230. Wilson Ornithological Society
http://www.wilsonsociety.org
Helping young avian (bird) students everywhere this society offers the *George A. Hall and Harold F. Mayfield Award*, the *Louis Agassiz Fuertes Award* and the *Paul A. Stewart Award.*

231.

Don't ignore scholarship books

Even though they lack the pizzazz of the Internet, scholarship books should not be overlooked. A good book provides a huge number of awards and an index to help you find them. There are a lot of scholarship books–and most are somewhat pricey–so we recommend that you head to your local library or counseling center and browse through their collection.

One that we recommend, and it is not an impartial opinion by any means, is our book, *The Ultimate Scholarship Book.* We wrote this book after getting frustrated with one too many traditional scholarship books that cost too much and gave too little. We wanted a book that listed awards that most students could win. We also wanted to make sure that we didn't just give you the best directory of scholarships but also that we taught you how to win. In *The Ultimate Scholarship Book* you'll find that the first part of the book is a detailed strategy guide on how to create a winning scholarship application. The second part of the book is a comprehensive scholarship directory to over 2,500 awards that you can apply to win.

Complementing our scholarship directory is our other scholarship book, *How to Write a Winning Scholarship Essay.* In this book you can read the essays of 30 scholarship winners and get tips directly from the scholarship judges who decide whether or not you win.

Regardless of whether you read our books, you should not ignore the value of traditional scholarship directories.

232.

Double your scholarship with Dollars for Scholars

There's only one thing better than winning a scholarship, and that is having that scholarship doubled. This might sound too good to be true, but trust us, it's the real deal. Sponsored by Scholarship America, Dollars for Scholars is a network of more than 1,100 community-based scholarship foundations. These organizations award a variety of scholarships. Some of the awards that you win will probably be through your local Dollars for Scholars chapter. If you win a scholarship through the Dollars for Scholars program and attend a college that is a Dollars for Scholars partner school then the school may automatically match your scholarship thereby doubling its value.

Your first step is to find a Dollars for Scholars foundation in your city. Contact it and see what scholarships are available and apply for those that match your background and interests. If you win, then check with your college to see if they will match your scholarship. Get started by visiting the Dollars for Scholars website at http://www.scholarshipamerica.org.

233.

Awards based on your ethnicity

A common misconception is ethnicity-based scholarships are only for minorities. While there are awards for minorities, there are also scholarships for many ethnicities that are not. When looking for one of these scholarships the best place to start is with organizations dedicated to supporting members of your ethnicity. The National Italian American Foundation or National Association for the Advancement of Colored People (NAACP) are good examples.

However, don't limit yourself only to these kinds of groups. If you are a minority, also look at companies and professional associations. Some have special scholarships to encourage underrepresented groups to enter a specific career or profession.

Keep in mind that there is no universal definition of who is a minority. Each scholarship defines which ethnic groups–and what qualifies you to be a member of an ethnic group–can apply. In general, the movement is toward "underrepresented" groups, which basically means ethnic groups that given their numbers within the general population are underrepresented in education or an industry. This definition means that an ethnic group that was considered a "minority" 10 years ago may no longer be considered one when it comes to a specific scholarship. It's best that you check eligibility requirements of the scholarship before you apply.

The following is a small sampling of ethnicity-based awards.

234. Actuarial Scholarships for Minority Students
http://www.beanactuary.org
This award is sponsored by the Casualty Actuarial Society/ Society of Actuaries. It provides awards for both undergraduate and graduate minority students who are interested in pursuing actuarial careers.

235. American Chemical Society Scholars Program
http://www.chemistry.org
Sponsored by the American Chemical Society, this program helps African American, Hispanic and Native American students who intend to major in chemistry or science.

236. American Indian Scholarship
http://www.dar.org
The National Society Daughters of the American Revolution provides this program to assist Native American students. There is no affiliation with DAR required.

237. American Society of Criminology Fellowships for Ethnic Minorities
http://www.asc41.com
The American Society of Criminology sponsors this program for African American, Asian American, Latino or Native American students who are majoring in criminology.

Aren't all scholarships based on financial need?

You could be the son or daughter of Bill Gates and still win a scholarship. It's true! The reason is because there are two kinds of scholarships available: need-based and merit-based.

As the name suggests, need-based scholarships are based on your financial need. To verify the level of your need, scholarship organizations may ask for tax returns or a copy of your Free Application for Federal Student Aid (FAFSA). Remember that the definition of need varies. Not all scholarships require extreme need. In fact, some organizations define families with incomes of up to $100,000 as needy. Also, it's important to know that need-based scholarships are not necessarily given to the most needy students. Many need-based scholarships also consider your academic and extracurricular achievement in addition to your financial situation.

On the other hand, merit-based scholarships do not take into account your financial status. Instead, they are based on other qualities such as your grades, involvement in activities, talents or other achievements. For these kinds of awards, it doesn't matter how many digits are in your family's income. You win these scholarships by showing that your background and achievements make you the most deserving of the award.

238. Armenian Students' Association of America Scholarship

http://www.asainc.org

This program is for students of Armenian descent who are college sophomores or beyond.

239. Asian American Journalists Association Scholarships

http://www.aaja.org

To increase the presence of historically underrepresented Asian Pacific American groups in journalism, this organization awards scholarships to students from backgrounds including Vietnamese, Cambodians, Hmong and other Southeast Asians, South

Asians and Pacific Islanders who are interested in journalism. Scholarships include the *Newhouse National Scholarship and Internship Awards*, the *Mary Moy Quan Ing Memorial Scholarship* and the *National AAJA General Scholarship Award*.

240. Asian and Pacific Islander American Scholarships
http://www.apiasf.org
This award supports Asian and Pacific Islander students who plan to be full-time college freshmen.

241. Brown Foundation Scholarships
http://www.brownvboard.org
The foundation assists minority high school seniors and college juniors who plan to enter careers in teaching.

242. Bureau of Indian Affairs High Education Grant
http://www.bia.gov
American Indian and Alaska Native undergraduate students who are members of a tribe or at least one-quarter degree Indian blood descendants may apply for these grants.

243. Cherokee Nation Undergraduate Scholarship Programs
http://www.cherokee.org
Applicants who are high school senior Cherokee Nation tribal members may apply for this award.

244. Council for Exceptional Children Ethnic Diversity Scholarship
http://www.cec.sped.org
Student CEC members from a minority ethnic background who are currently pursuing degrees in special education can apply for this award.

245. Gates Millennium Scholars Program
http://www.gmsp.org
African American, American Indian/Alaska Native, Asian Pacific Islander American or Hispanic American students can apply for this program.

246. Gillette/National Urban League Scholarship and Intern Program for Minority Students

http://www.nul.org

This program helps outstanding African American undergraduates majoring in engineering and business fields.

247. Hellenic Times Scholarship Fund

http://www.htsfund.org

This scholarship supports undergraduate or graduate students of Greek descent between the ages of 17 and 30.

248. Hispanic College Fund Scholarship

http://www.hispanicfund.org

Hispanic students pursuing their bachelor's degree and majoring in a business- or technology-related field may apply for this award.

249. Hispanic Heritage Awards Foundation

http://www.hispanicheritage.org

Hispanic American youth may apply for scholarships in one of these specific disciplines: Academic Excellence, Sports, the Arts, Literature/Journalism, Mathematics, Leadership/Community Service and Science and Technology.

250. Hispanic Outlook Magazine Scholarship Fund

http://www.hispanicoutlook.com

Hispanic high school seniors can apply for this scholarship.

251. Hispanic Scholarship Fund (HSF)

http://www.hsf.net

Students of Hispanic heritage may apply to this program that has awarded more than 45,000 scholarships over the past 25 years.

252. Japanese American Citizens League

http://www.jacl.org

This organization aids student members with various awards including the *Hawigara Student Aid Award*, the *Japanese American Citizens League Creative and Performing Arts Award*, the *Japanese American Citizens League Entering Freshman Award*, the *Japanese American Citizens League Graduate Award*, the *Japanese American*

Citizens League Law Scholarship and the *Japanese American Citizens League Undergraduate Award.*

253. Kosciuszko Tuition Scholarship Program
http://www.thekf.org
Students of Polish descent may apply for this scholarship from the Kosciuszko Foundation.

254. League of United Latin American Citizens Scholarship Fund
http://www.lulac.org
Hispanic students who have applied or are enrolled in a college, university or graduate school may apply for an award.

255. League of United Latin American Citizens GM Fund
http://lulac.org/programs/education/scholarships/
If you are a full-time minority college student majoring in courses that will lead to an engineering career you can apply for an award from the *GM Fund.*

256. National Action Council for Minorities in Engineering
http://www.nacme.org
This group offers a variety of scholarships and pre-college programs including the *United Space Alliance Scholarship* and the *3M Corporation Scholarship.*

257. National Association for the Advancement of Colored People (NAACP)
http://www.naacp.org
The NAACP awards over 100 scholarships each year. Some of the awards include the *Earl Graves Scholarship*, the *Agnes Jones Scholarship*, the *Louis Stokes Scholarship*, the *Sutton Scholarship*, the *Roy Wilkins Scholarship* and the *Willems Scholarship.* You can download applications from the website.

258. National Association of Black Accountants Scholarship Program
http://www.nabainc.org
This program is for African Americans and other minorities who intend to enter accounting or finance professions.

259. National Association of Black Journalists Scholarship Program
http://www.nabj.org
This scholarship supports African American students who are planning to pursue careers in journalism.

260. National Association of Hispanic Journalists Scholarships
http://www.nahj.org
Scholarships include the *Cristina Saralegüi Scholarship*, the *NAHJ Scholarship* and the *Newhouse Scholarship*.

261. National Association of Minority Engineering Program Administrators
http://www.namepa.org
To support minority students who want to become engineers, this association offers the *NAMEPA Scholarship Program*.

262. National Black Police Association
http://www.blackpolice.org
The *Alphonso Deal Scholarship Award* is given to high school seniors who are planning to study law enforcement.

263. National Society of Black Engineers
http://www.nsbe.org
Encouraging black students to enter engineering, this organization offers a variety of scholarships and competitions for students of nearly all levels.

264. Native American Journalists Association Scholarship
http://www.naja.com
This award is for Native American students pursuing journalism degrees.

265. Order Sons of Italy in America
http://www.osia.org
Applicants must be enrolled in an undergraduate or graduate program and be of Italian descent.

**What happens if I find too many scholarships?
How do I know which ones to apply for?**

Since there are tens of thousands of scholarships available, your problem may not be finding awards but deciding which ones to apply for and which you have the best chance of winning. Although there is no way to predict if you will win a scholarship, there is one method you can use to select those that fit you best and therefore offer you the best chance of winning.

The key is to realize that almost every scholarship organization has a mission or goal for giving away its money. Few groups give away free money for no reason. For example, a nature group might sponsor a scholarship with the goal of promoting conservation and encouraging students to be environmentally conscious. To this end the group will reward students who have demonstrated a concern for the environment and have some plan to contribute to this cause in the future.

Understanding the mission of the scholarship is important because it will clue you in to the kind of student the organization is looking for. If you have the background, interests and accomplishments that match this mission and are able to convey that in your application, you have a good chance of winning the award.

266. Organization of Chinese Americans

http://www.ocanational.org

This organization offers various scholarships for African American, Asian American, Hispanic American and Native American high school students including the *Lead Summer Program*, the *OCA Avon College Scholarship*, the *OCA National Essay Contest* and the *OCA/UPS Gold Mountain Scholarship*.

267. Public Relations Student Society of America-Multicultural Affairs Scholarship Program

http://www.prssa.org

Students who are of African American, Hispanic, Asian, Native American, Alaskan Native or Pacific Islander ancestry and studying communications may apply for this award.

268. Ron Brown Scholar Program
http://www.ronbrown.org
This program awards scholarships to academically talented and highly motivated African American high school seniors.

269. Scholarships for Disadvantaged Students in Health Professions
http://www.hrsa.gov/loanscholarships/
The Bureau of Health Professions offers scholarships for students from disadvantaged background who also have financial need and are enrolled in health or nursing programs. Individual schools select the scholarship recipients. Contact your financial aid office for details.

270. Society of Hispanic Professional Engineers
http://www.shpe.org
Hispanic students studying math, science and engineering disciplines may apply for a scholarship.

271. The National Italian American Foundation
http://www.niaf.org
Italian American students who demonstrate outstanding potential and high academic achievement or students of any ethnic background who are majoring or minoring in the Italian language or Italian American studies can apply for this group's scholarship.

272. Thurgood Marshall Scholarship Fund
http://www.thurgoodmarshallfund.org
Students enrolled or planning to enroll as full-time students at one of the 45 historically black public colleges and universities, who have demonstrated a commitment to academic excellence and community service and who show financial need can apply for this award.

273. U.S. Pan Asian American Chamber of Commerce
http://www.uspaacc.com
Asian American students may apply for a variety of awards including: the *Asian American Scholarship Fund Award*, the *Yue-Sai Kan Scholarship*, the *Bernadette Wong-Yu Scholarship*, the *Bruce Lee Scholarship* (no martial arts skills required), the *Cary C. and Debra*

Y.C. Wu Scholarship, the *Drs. Poh Shien and Judy Young Scholarship*, the *Jackie Chan Scholarship*, the *Ruth Mu-Lan Chu and James S.C. Chao Scholarship* and the *Telamon Scholarship*.

274. United Negro College Fund Scholarships
http://www.uncf.org
Applicants must be African American, have a minimum 2.5 GPA and must have unmet financial need. The UNCF offers a variety of scholarships and grants.

275.

Scholarships for a disability
Many organizations that work on behalf of specific physical or mental disabilities offer scholarship programs. Contact them directly or visit their websites to see what scholarships are available. The Easter Seal Society, for example, offers scholarships through local chapters for students with disabilities. Contact your local Easter Seal Rehabilitation Center to see what scholarships are available in your area. The same is true of most of the other organizations. Here are a few to get you started.

For the hearing impaired:

276. Alexander Graham Bell Association
Alexander Graham Bell Association Scholarship
http://www.agbell.org

277. Children of Deaf Adults, International
Millie Brother Scholarship
http://www.coda-international.org

278. EAR Foundation
Minnie Pearl Scholarship
http://www.earfoundation.org

279. National Association of the Deaf
William C. Stokoe Scholarship
http://www.nad.org

280. National Fraternal Society of the Deaf
Deaf Scholarship
http://www.nfsd.com

281. Travelers Protective Association
TPA Scholarship Trust for the Deaf and Near Deaf
http://www.tpahq.org/scholarshiptrust/

For the visually impaired:

282. American Foundation for the Blind
Ferdinand Torres and Karen D. Carsel Memorial Scholarship
http://www.afb.org

283. Association for Education and Rehabilitation of the Blind and Visually Impaired
William and Dorothy Ferrell Scholarship
http://www.aerbvi.org

284. Christian Record Services
CRS Scholarship for the Legally Blind
http://www.christianrecord.org

285. National Federation of Music Clubs
The NFMC Hinda Honigman Award for the Blind
http://www.nfmc-music.org

286. National Federation of the Blind
National Federation of the Blind Scholarship
http://www.nfb.org

For physical disabilities:

287. Andre Sobel River of Life Foundation
Andre Sobel Award
http://www.andreriveroflife.org

288. Bank of America
Bank of America ADA Abilities Scholarship Program
http://www.scholarshipprograms.org

289. Chair Scholars
Chair Scholars Scholarship for the Physically Challenged
http://www.chairscholars.org

290. Microsoft Scholarships for Students with Disabilities
Microsoft's award is aimed at current college students who are interested in entering the software industry.
Website: https://www.microsoft.com/en-us/diversity/programs/microsoftdisabilityscholarship.aspx

291. Pfizer
Pfizer Epilepsy Scholarship
http://www.epilepsy-scholarship.com

292. Spina Bifida Association of America
SBAA Scholarship Fund
http://www.spinabifidaassociation.org

For learning disabilities:

293. International Dyslexia Association
The IDA offers various scholarships through their local associations.
http://www.interdys.org

How do I get a scholarship application?

Scholarship applications are typically offered online. Some are available for download. Then, you print the application and mail it to the organization or complete the application electronically. Other applications are available to complete online. In some cases, applications are available on paper and you may request them by mail or from your counselor.

294. National Center for Learning Disabilities
Anne Ford Scholarship Program
http://www.ncld.org

295. The P. Buckley Moss Society
Ann and Matt Harbison Scholarship
http://www.mosssociety.org

296. Shire ADHD College Scholarship Program
This program assists students who have been diagnosed with ADHD.
http://www.shireadhdscholarship.com

297. VSA Arts
Young Soloists Awards are for student musicians with mental or physical disabilities.
http://vsarts.org

298.

Awards based on personal challenges and hardships

If you've overcome personal challenges or hardships, you can certainly describe this in your scholarship applications no matter what the award. Almost every scholarship judge will be impressed if you have overcome obstacles and reached your goals despite personal challenges. However, there are a few organizations that are dedicated specifically to recognizing students who have overcome significant challenges.

Two of the better known are the *American Cancer Society College Scholarship Program* and the *Horatio Alger Association Scholarship Program*. The *American Cancer Society College Scholarship Program* offers scholarships for students (usually under the age of 25) who are cancer survivors. Each program is run by a local ACS organization. You can find your local ACS at http://www.cancer.org.

The *Horatio Alger Association Scholarship Program* is for students who have overcome major obstacles in their life, are committed to using their college degrees in service to others and demonstrate financial need. Visit http://www.horatioalger.com to receive more information.

When you write about hardships that you've faced in your application, remember that you need to do more than just describe the challenge. You also need to explain how you have survived or overcome the challenge and what you have learned from the experience. Scholarship winners are not those who have faced the most difficult challenges, but those who have encountered obstacles and grown stronger from the experience.

299.

Turn your hobbies and talents into scholarship gold

Whether it's playing basketball or backgammon, we all have interests and hobbies that we pursue outside of the classroom. While we think of these as enjoyable diversions, sometimes they can also be the basis for winning a scholarship. The way to find out if your interest has a related scholarship is to inquire with organized enthusiast groups.

For example, if your hobby is short-wave radio, check out the website of the Amateur Radio Relay League at http://www.arrlf.org. You'll find that this group offers more than a dozen scholarships.

If you are a member of your school band, you might subscribe to *School Band and Orchestra Magazine.* This publication (http://www. sbomagazine.com) sponsors an essay competition for students in grades 4 through 12 for a scholarship.

If you do some digging around your interests and hobbies, chances are you'll find groups and organizations that want to reward students like you.

300.

Scholarship organizations love leaders

You might be a leader and not even know it. While there are many scholarships for leaders, it's amazing how many students don't think they are a leader simply because they don't have the appropriate title such as "president" or "secretary." Being a leader is not just about being elected. You can be a leader simply for organizing your peers. If you have ever organized an event or special project, that is certainly an example of leadership.

One of the most well-known leadership scholarships is the *Principals Leadership Award Scholarship* sponsored by the National Association of Secondary School Principals (http://www.nassp.org) and Herff Jones (http://www.herff-jones.com). Principals nominate high school senior student leaders based on their leadership skills, participation in service organizations, achievements in the arts and sciences, work experience and academic record. There are 150 students from all 50 states who win $1,000 scholarships.

Most scholarships whether they say so or not value leadership. In all of your applications and interviews you should cite examples of your

---

How do I describe my accomplishments to impress the scholarship judges?

Winning a scholarship is about impressing the judges and showing them why you are the best candidate. Your accomplishments, activities, talents and awards all help to prove that you are the best fit. Since you will probably list your activities on the application form, you can use your essay to expand on one or two of the most important. However, don't just parrot back what is on your application. Use the opportunity to focus on a specific accomplishment, provide detail and to put it into the proper context. Listing on your application that you were a stage manager for a play does not explain that you also had to design and build all of the sets in a week. The essay allows you to expand on an achievement to demonstrate its significance.

leadership skills when possible. Remember, you do not have to be in an elected office to be a leader. Any time you have taken the initiative to organize an activity, you have shown leadership.

301.

Turn your community service into scholarship dollars

Whether you collect canned goods for the homeless or sing for lonely senior citizens, volunteer work makes you feel good. This is a noble use of your time which can lead to scholarships that recognize your commitment to your community.

Many students mistake community service as being measured by hours spent per week or doing traditional service club activities. But serving the community can take many forms including being a coach of a little league team or helping to tutor at a community center. What's more important than the number of hours you serve is the contribution that you make. Don't assume that you cannot complete for a service-based scholarship just because you haven't committed thousands of hours.

AmeriCorps sponsors the *Presidential Freedom Scholarships* to promote and recognize leadership in service and citizenship. Applicants must be high school juniors or seniors who have contributed at least 100 hours of service within the past year, demonstrate outstanding citizenship through their service and participation in other community activities and plan to attend an eligible institute of higher learning. Learn more by visiting the Americorps website at: http://www.americorps.gov.

302.

You don't have to be a superstar athlete to win a scholarship

You might think you need to be the next Stephen Curry or Hope Solo to win an athletic scholarship. While superior athletic skills certainly wouldn't hurt, the truth is that you don't have to be an athletic superstar to win a scholarship. Naturally you need to be gifted to get an athletic scholarship to play football for the University of Southern California or Ohio State since they are top ranked teams, but you do not necessarily have to be the best for many other college teams.

Even at schools with strong athletic programs, the sport that you play may not be as competitive. This means that the caliber of athlete they are looking for will be much different than for the nationally ranked programs. Many students have won partial or even full athletic scholarships even though they were not even the best athletes at their high school.

The key to getting an athletic scholarship is to be proactive about contacting the coaches at the colleges you are interested in before you apply. Send an email or letter to coaches and tell them that you are a prospective applicant and are also interested in playing on their team. Be ready to send a portfolio of your athletic accomplishments and also make sure to get a letter from your current coach that will attest not only to your abilities but also to your character as an athlete. To find which schools offer athletic programs in your area, visit the NCAA website at http://www.ncaa.org.

Besides athletic scholarships from the colleges, you can also apply for private athletic scholarships from various sporting associations. Here are a few of the more popular ones, but don't forget about the local associations in your area either:

303. Foot Locker
Foot Locker Scholar Athletes
https://footlockerscholarathletes.com

304. Harness Horse Youth Foundation
Harness Racing Scholarship
http://www.hhyf.org

305. Ice Skating Institute of America (ISIA)
ISIA Education Foundation Scholarship
http://www.skateisi.com

306. National Amateur Baseball Federation
Ronald and Irene McMinn Scholarship
http://www.nabf.com

307. National Archery Association
NAA College Scholarship
http://www.usarchery.org

308. National Athletic Trainers' Association
NATA Scholarship
http://www.nata.org

309. National Rifle Association
NRA Junior Member Scholarship
http://www.nrahq.org

310. Our World-Underwater Scholarship Society
North American Rolex Scholarship
http://www.owuscholarship.org

311. Pop Warner
All-American Scholar Program
http://www.popwarner.com

312. Stonehouse Publishing Company
Stonehouse Golf Youth Scholarship
http://www.stonehousegolf.com

313. Wendy's Restaurants
Wendy's High School Heisman Award
http://www.wendyshighschoolheisman.com

314. Women's Sports Foundation
Linda Riddle/SGMA Scholarship
http://www.womenssportsfoundation.org

315.

Ace your college applications to get more scholarships

You may not realize that your college applications are also scholarship applications. If the colleges really want you, then they will not only offer you admission but will also give you an automatic scholarship. Even if you know that you are a definite admission for the college you are applying to, spend the time and effort to create an outstanding application. That might be the difference between simply getting admitted and getting admitted with a $10,000 scholarship.

If you want to learn more about how to ace your college admission applications, we recommend our books, *Get into Any College* and *Accepted! 50 Successful College Admission Essays*.

316.

Help the colleges help you by providing everything they may need to give you a scholarship

When you apply for a scholarship from a college they may ask you to only complete a simple application form. However, you should always include an essay and resume. The reason is that when the scholarship committee reviews your application they may find that you are also qualified for another scholarship from the college. However, this scholarship may require an essay. If you include an essay it will make it very easy for the college to award you the scholarship. You may be surprised to learn that colleges are always looking for students who match their various scholarship programs. Help them help you by giving them everything they would need to award you a scholarship.

317.

Don't let the colleges take away your scholarship money

When you win a scholarship, you have to report it to your college. Unfortunately, sometimes a college will decrease your financial aid by the amount of scholarship money that you win. Not fair, you say? You're absolutely right! If this happens to you, immediately contact the organization that gave you the scholarship and explain the situation. Some scholarship organizations have policies against giving an award to a student if the college will adjust their financial aid package. With the scholarship organization on your side, approach the college financial aid office. In most cases the financial aid office will back down rather than see you forfeit the scholarship.

If the college insists on adjusting your financial aid package, ask that they lower your "self-help" (e.g. student loan) amounts rather than grants. It's much better for you to have to borrow less in loans anyway. Be firm in making your case and be sure to point out to the college that their policy gives you little incentive to apply for any scholarships in the future.

If none of these strategies work, you should still take the scholarship since the scholarship is guaranteed while any financial aid grants are subject to availability of the funds. Even if you get a grant in one year you might not receive the same amount the next year. But a scholarship, if it's renewable, will pay you the same amount every year.

318.

Strange and offbeat scholarships

You've heard the rumors. Somewhere there is a scholarship just for left-handed students. Maybe you heard from a friend of a friend that you can get a scholarship for being tall. While careful investigation reveals that even though there is a scholarship for lefties (given to students at Juniata College in Huntingdon, Pennsylvania) just because you are left-handed does not mean you automatically win. You still have to beat out all of the other talented lefties. We're sure that once you start your scholarship search you'll find plenty of your own strange scholarships.

Here are a few offbeat scholarships to give you an idea of what's out there. Our point in sharing these awards is to inspire you. No matter what your background, talent or achievements, you can find a scholarship that fits. These scholarships prove it.

319. Asparagus Club Scholarships
https://www.nationalgrocers.org
This program has awarded more than $850,000 in scholarships to rising college juniors and seniors and graduate students who are earning a degree in a business, food management or other related major leading to a career in the independent retail grocery industry. A love of asparagus is not required!

320. Collegiate Inventors Competition
http://www.collegiateinventors.org
Have an idea for a new invention? This scholarship supports exploration in invention, science and technology.

321. David Letterman Scholarship
http://www.bsu.edu
He may be most famous for his Top 10 Lists, but David Letterman also has a scholarship for telecommunications students at his alma mater, Ball State University.

322. Duck Calling Contest
http://www.stuttgartarkansas.org
Quack! Do you have a talent for duck calling? The Chick and Sophie Major Memorial Contest awards the country's best duck calls.

323. Duct Tape Stuck at Prom Scholarship
http://www.stuckatprom.com
The makers of "Duck"

brand duct tape sponsor this award. The prize is a $6,000 award for the couple that goes to their high school prom in the most original attire made from duct tape, which comes in 17 colors!

324. Little People of America Scholarship
http://www.lpaonline.org
You may have heard of the scholarships for tall people. There are also scholarships for those who are short in stature. You must be no taller than 4'10" and have a medically diagnosed form of dwarfism.

325. Magic Scholarship
http://www.gamershelpinggamers.org
Who knew that playing a card game could win you a scholarships? If you enjoy the *Magic The Gathering* card game then you could enter their annual Junior Super Series competition held in cities around the country. Winners earn thousands of dollars in college scholarships.

326. Marbles Scholarship
http://www.nationalmarblestournament.org
You can win money for almost any interest. During a four-day tournament, "mibsters," or marble shooters, compete in more than 1,200 marble games to win scholarship awards.

327. Million-Dollar Name
http://www.luc.edu
Loyola University in Chicago offers a full-tuition, four-year scholarship to any student who is Catholic and whose last name is Zolp. The last name must appear on both the birth and confirmation certificate.

328. National Candy Technologists Scholarship Program
http://www.aactcandy.org/aactscholarship.asp
Do you love candy? If you have a demonstrated interest in confectionary technology, this may be the scholarship for you.

329. National Potato Council Scholarship
http://www.nationalpotatocouncil.org

Are you thinking of majoring in french fries? Okay, not really. But if you are a graduate student in agribusiness in a field that supports the potato industry, you could win $5,000.

330. Pokemon Scholarships
https://www.pokemon.com/us/play-pokemon/worlds/2018/prizes/
Your Pokemon collection in that old shoe box can finally help you pay for college! Scholarships are given to winners in the national and world championships.

331. Tall Student Scholarship
http://www.tall.org
Awarded each year by Tall Club International, applicants for this $1,000 scholarship must be over 6'2" if you're male or 5'10" if you're female. Tall Club International has more than 200 local clubs across the U.S., many of which offer their own scholarships. The award can be used at any college to study any major.

Contests For Students

Do You Feel Lucky?

Does the word "contest" conjure up images of Ed McMahon knocking on your door, oversized check in hand? While there are contests based on luck, there are also contests that focus on your abilities within a specific skill—such as art, writing or music.

Unlike scholarship competitions, these contests for students are based on just one criterion—such as your ability to write a short story or paint a picture. Things like grades, test scores and extracurricular activities have no meaning in these contests. You are judged purely on your submission or performance.

What's nice about these contests is that they are open only to students, which greatly reduces the competition and increases your chance of winning. Unlike Publisher's Clearinghouse millions of people are not entering.

The following are some of the larger contests that students can enter. Be sure that you also check locally since we found many contests that are limited to students in specific cities and states that we didn't have the s p a c e to include. Just like scholarships, any backyard contests that you find will give you the best odds of winning.

And just for fun we also included a few contests that are based purely on chance for those of you who are feeling lucky.

Contests For Writers And Poets

Unlike scholarships that require an essay as part of the overall competition, in these contests the essay is the competition. Winners are selected based only on their essays. You'll find that many of these competitions are open to students younger than high school seniors and are a great way to get started earning some money.

332. American Fire Sprinkler Association Essay Contest
http://www.firesprinkler.org
You don't have to be an expert on fire sprinklers to enter this contest, but you do have to write an essay on the importance of fire sprinklers. Here's a sample of a recent essay question: "How do fire sprinklers function and where are they required in your community?" Winners receive $1,000 to $3,000.

333. Ayn Rand Essay Contest–*Anthem*
http://www.aynrand.org/contests/
During the course of high school most of you will read something by Ayn Rand. If you do there is an amazing essay contest based on a number of her books. This essay contest is based on Ayn Rand's *Anthem* and is for students in the eighth, ninth or 10th grade. The first prize is $2,000. There are also additional runner-up prizes.

334. Ayn Rand Essay Contest–*Atlas Shrugged*
http://www.aynrand.org/contests/
If you are in the 12th grade or college and have read *Atlas Shrugged* you can enter this essay contest. The first prize is $5,000, and there are also three second prizes worth $1,000.

335. Ayn Rand Essay Contest–*The Fountainhead*
http://www.aynrand.org/contests/
If you're a junior or senior in high school you can enter this essay contest that is based on Ayn Rand's *The Fountainhead.* The first prize is $10,000.

336. Ayn Rand Essay Contest–*We the Living*
http://www.aynrand.org/contests/
High school sophomores, juniors and seniors are eligible to enter this essay contest that is based on Ayn Rand's *We the Living.* The first prize is $3,000.

337. Guidepost Young Writers Contest
http://www.guideposts.com
To enter you must write a first-person story about a memorable or moving experience. This contest is for high school juniors or seniors. Prizes range from $250 to $10,000.

338. Holocaust Remembrance Project

http://holocaust.hklaw.com/

This is a national essay contest for high school students designed to encourage the study of the Holocaust. The project also serves as a living memorial to the victims of the Holocaust. First-place winners receive a scholarship of up to $5,000.

339. Inverness Corporation "Is All Ears" Essay Contest

http://www.invernesscorp.com

What do Arnold Schwarzenegger and Oprah Winfrey have in common? Not much except that either could be your answer to this contest question. Open to all high school students ages 14 to 19, this contest asks the question: "If you had the ear of any special person, famous or not, what would you tell them and why?" Answers must be a terse 150 words or less. Prizes range from $1,000 to $5,000.

340. John F. Kennedy Profile in Courage Essay Contest

http://www.jfklibrary.org/Education/Profile-in-Courage-Essay-Contest.aspx

This essay contest is open to all students in grades 9 to 12. Each year $6,500 in prizes are awarded. You must write an essay of no more than 1,000 words on one of the provided essay questions. Visit the contest website for official rules and to get this year's questions.

341. L. Ron Hubbard Writers of the Future

http://www.writersofthefuture.com

This is a science fiction short story contest for amateur writers. Prizes range from $500 to $4,000.

342. Mensa Education & Research Foundation Scholarship Program

http://www.mensafoundation.org/scholarships

The brainiacs at Mensa have created an award program that is based only on your written essays. You don't have to be a member of Mensa, and grades and financial need are not a consideration. The scholarship program is managed by each local Mensa group, and you must apply through your local Mensa organization.

343. National Council of Teachers of English Student Writing Awards

http://www.ncte.org

The NCTE sponsors several writing awards including the *Achievement Awards in Writing* that recognizes the writing abilities of high school students. You must be nominated by your school for this award competition. The group also sponsors the *Promising Young Writers Program* that is open to students in the eighth grade. Visit the NCTE website for more information and current deadlines.

344. National Peace Essay Contest

http://www.usip.org/category/course-type/national-peace-essay-contest

Students in grades 9 to 12 may enter an essay into this contest, which as the name suggests is about world peace. You must be sponsored by a school, school club, youth group, community group or religious organization with an adult advisor.

345. National Schools Project Young Poets Contest

http://www.youngpoets.org/Contest.htm

Calling all aspiring poets. This contest recognizes young poetry writers (grades K-12.) To enter you must submit an original poem of 21 lines or less. Winners divide more than $70,000 in prizes.

346. Optimist International Essay Contest

http://www.optimist.org

This essay contest awards $44,000 annually in scholarships. Applicants must be under 19 years of age and submit short essays on the topic of freedom. Begin the process by submitting your essay to your local Optimist Club. You can find your local club through the Optimist Club's website.

347. Playwright Discovery Award

http://education.kennedy-center.org//education/vsa/

Students in grades 6 to 12 can win a scholarship for creating an original one-act play script.

348. Power Poetry Scholarships

http://www.powerpoetry.org

Power Poetry offers scholarship contests year-round for high school and college students who submit poems on provided topics. Recent topics include writing about what has shaped you this past year.

349. Scholastic Art and Writing Awards
http://www.artandwriting.org
Students in grades 7 to 12 can enter this competition. You can read past winners' essays online as well as download an application and current contest rules.

350. Signet Classic Student Scholarship Essay Contest
http://us.penguingroup.com/static/pages/services-academic/essayhome.html
The prospect of winning a scholarship is one way to get you to read literary classics. High school juniors and seniors can enter this contest by writing essays on topics related to literature classics. A recent competition was based on Mary Shelley's book *Frankenstein*. Five winners win $1,000 scholarships that can be used toward college.

351. The Laws of Life Essay Contest
http://www.lawsoflife.org
Unlike most essay contests, this one does not provide a topic. You are encouraged to write from your heart. However, you should understand what this group is about and the principles that it advocates. The contest is open to all elementary, high school and college students. You can learn more about the Laws of Life organization and get more information on how to enter online.

352. UNA-USA National High School Essay Contest on the United Nations
http://www.unausa.org (Click on "Education" and then click on "Programs.")
It's time for your best Miss America impression. What is an issue of global concern to you? This

annual essay contest gives high school students in grades 9 to 12 the opportunity to address an issue of significant global concern. Essays must be 1,500 words or less. You must submit your essay to your local United Nations Association Chapter, which you can find on the organization's website. The first prize is $1,000, and naturally, your essay needs to be a little more thought provoking than a 30-second Miss America answer.

Contests For Performing Arts

If you dream of seeing your names in lights and are fearless of the stage then these contests are for you. The following contests are for musicians, thespians and students involved in speech competitions. Most require submitting an original work such as a speech or composition, and most of the music competitions are performance based.

353. American Society of Composers, Authors and Publishers
http://www.ascapfoundation.org/awards.html
The ASCAP foundation offers several music composition competitions including the *Young Jazz Composer Awards*, the *Heineken Music Initiative* for R&B songwriters, the *Morton Gould Young Composer Awards* and the *Rudolf Nissim Prize*. In addition, you can find a list of music scholarships administered by individual high schools, colleges and conservatories on the website.

354. Arts Recognition and Talent Search (ARTS)
http://www.youngarts.org
If you are a talented high school senior, you can apply to the

Where can I find more contests for writers?

If after applying to the writing contests in this chapter you still have more words in you, here is a writer's contests directory with more competitions. Note that these are not specifically for students, but most are open to writers of any age. To see the list just surf on over to https://thewritelife.com/writing-contests/.

National YoungArts Foundation program. The YoungArts program identifies young artists in dance, film and video, jazz music, photography, theater visual arts, voice and writing. Each year YoungArts awards more than $3 million in college scholarships. YoungArts program participants can also be named an YoungArts Finalist to compete for the honor of being named Presidential Scholars in the Arts. Also, the jazz, music and voice discipline winners can attend the YoungArts Week in Miami and win additional prizes worth up to $25,000.

355. BMI Foundation Awards

http://www.bmifoundation.org

The BMI Foundation offers a variety of scholarship programs including the *John Lennon Scholarship Program*, which was established by Yoko Ono in 1997. This program recognizes songwriters in any genre who are between the ages of 15 and 25. The *Pete Carpenter Fellowship* gives aspiring TV and film composers

---

How can I make a recording of my performance to send to one of these contests?

Many music and vocal contests require a CD or electronic file. It's very important that you don't skimp on this since no matter how talented you are if you record in a noisy room with a dog barking in the background, it will affect the quality of your performance. But you don't have to shell out hundreds of dollars to rent a studio either.

Consider these no-cost options. Visit your community college and speak to a professor in the applied music department. Tell the professor what you want to do and ask if he or she will let you borrow the recording studio for an hour. Even easier, if you have friends who are in college they can probably hook you up with another student who has access to the campus music studio. Another option is to visit your local public access cable station. They should be listed in the phone book. You can get a file made of your performance using their professional sound equipment. You might even be able to get your school's A/V club to help out. As you can see there are a lot of free options for recording your performance.

the opportunity to work with composer Mike Post at his studio in Los Angeles and includes a $2,000 stipend for travel and expenses. The fellowship is open to any composer under the age of 35. The BMI Foundation also sponsors its own *Student Composer Awards*, which are for young composers of classical music. You must be a high school or college student or studying under a music teacher and under the age of 26.

356. Chopin Foundation
http://www.chopin.org
This program is available to any pianists age 14 to 17 who are enrolled in secondary or undergraduate institutions as full-time students.

357. Dizzy Feet Foundation
http://dizzyfeetfoundation.org/scholarships/information/
This program is open to students at least 15 years old who are attending an accredited dance school or institution. Awards of up to $10,000 are given.

358. Donna Reed Performing Arts Scholarships
http://www.donnareed.org
The Donna Reed Festival and Workshops for the Performing Arts includes categories for acting, vocal and musical theater. Three $4,000 scholarships are awarded to high school seniors, which may be used at any college.

359. Educational Theatre Association Thespian Scholarships
http://www.edta.org
Each year this association gives away more than $25,000 in scholarships. To apply for an award you must be a high school senior, be active in the International Thespian Society and plan to continue your thespian education in college. A number of competitions are held at the International Thespian Festival. You must audition for the competition. Another program awards money through your state thespian conference. Contact your state thespian director for details. You can learn more about the scholarships and find a directory of state directors at the EDTA website.

360. Glenn Miller Scholarship Competition

http://www.glennmiller.org

You'll be relieved to know that you don't have to look or sound like Glenn Miller to win this competition. The Glenn Miller Birthplace Society offers four scholarships each year for instrumentalists and vocalists to recognize promising young musicians in any field of applied music. To enter you must be a high school senior or college freshman who intends to make music a part of your career. You must also submit a tape of your musical performance.

361. Joseph S. Rumbaugh Oration Contest

http://www.sar.org/youth/rumbaugh.html

Attention history buffs! The National Society of the Sons of the American Revolution sponsors an oratorical scholarship for high school sophomores through seniors. The topic must address an event or person in the Revolutionary War showing the relationship to America today. You compete through your local or state chapters. Find a list of local chapters on the website. Prizes range from $200 to $3,000.

362. Optimist Oratorical Contest

http://www.optimist.org/e/member/scholarships4.cfm

If you're the type of person who likes public speaking, this scholarship is for you. Students who are younger than 16 years old may enter this oratory competition through their local Optimist Club. Each year more than $159,000 is awarded in scholarships. Prizes range from $500 to $1,500.

363. Young Artist Competition

http://www.minnesotaorchestra.org

Founded in 1956, this program is sponsored by WAMSO (Minnesota Orchestra Volunteer Association) and is designed to encourage musical education. Musicians do not need to be residents of Minnesota but must be under the age of 26 and meet all other eligibility requirements. You must also submit a tape or CD of your performance to be judged in the preliminary rounds. The final round is a live performance competition at Macalester College in St. Paul.

364. Young Concert Artists International
http://www.yca.org
Each year this group holds a competition in which four winners are selected to receive a $5,000 award and perform in the Young Concert Artists Series in New York, Boston and Washington, D.C.

Contests For Artists

Let's shed the starving artist stereotype here. If you are an aspiring artist, there are ways to earn some recognition and bank some future cash for college. There are a number of competitions that require you to submit your artwork (or a photograph of your artwork.) Be sure to look at the judging requirements of each contest since they can give you valuable hints about what the judges are looking for in a winning entry.

365. Christophers
http://www.christophers.org
With its motto, "It's better to light one candle than to curse the darkness," the Christophers sponsors an annual poster contest with prizes of up to $1,000. The contest is open to high school students.

366. College Photographer of the Year
http://www.nppa.org
Sponsored by the National Press Photographers Association, this award supports student work in photojournalism.

367. Federal Duck Jr. Stamp Competition
http://duckstamps.fws.gov
All entrants must be over the age of 18 and must design an original stamp featuring an eligible duck. The national winners receive scholarships up to $4,000, and the first place national winner's design is made into a stamp. Pretty cool.

368. Images of Freedom Student Photography Contest
http://www.abanet.org
Students between the ages of 12 and 18 may submit original photos that depict the Law Day theme. Prizes include national recognition, inclusion in a photo exhibit, a U.S. savings bond and educational materials.

369. National Sculpture Society Scholarship
http://www.nationalsculpture.org
College students of figurative or representational sculpture can apply for these $2,000 scholarships for emerging artists. Scholarships are paid directly to the college through which the student applies.

370. Scholastic Art and Writing Awards
http://www.artandwriting.org
Young writers and artists in grades 7 to 12 can enter this competition sponsored by Scholastic. You can view the winning entries from previous years online.

371. Worldstudio Foundation
http://www.worldstudio.org
This foundation supports undergraduate and graduate students majoring in fine or commercial arts, design or architecture who are minorities or who have financial need.

Contests Of Chance

Some people are born lucky. We have an aunt who always seems to be a magnet for slot machine jackpots in Vegas. On the other hand, one of the luckiest days that I (Kelly) had was when I was a kid and won a call-in radio contest. The prize? I got to ride on top of an elephant at the circus. Unfortunately, unlike the prizes of the following contests, that elephant ride didn't help me pay for college. If you consider yourself lucky or just feel lucky you might want to enter a few contests that are only open to students. On the positive side these contests are very easy to enter. On the negative side your fate is totally beyond your control.

372. eCampusTours $1,000 Scholarship Drawing
http://www.ecampustours.com
You can win one of ten $1,000 scholarships by registering on this website.

373. Next Step Magazine
http://www.nextstepmagazine.com
Winners are randomly selected for this magazine's $5,000 scholarship. You must be 14 years or older to enter.

374. Off to College Scholarship Sweepstakes
http://www.suntrusteducation.com/sweeps
Every two weeks a high school senior wins a $1,000 scholarship and $250 SunTrust gift card in this drawing.

375. Sallie Mae $1,000 Scholarship Drawing
http://www.salliemae.com/scholarships
Each month Sallie Mae selects a registered user to receive a $1,000 scholarship. Registration is free and you also get access to some cool resources such as a free scholarship search.

376. SuperCollege Scholarship
http://www.supercollege.com
Sign up to win this $1,500 scholarship awarded through a random drawing. It doesn't get easier than that!

377. U.S. Bank Internet Scholarship Program
http://www.usbank.com/studentbanking
If you're a high school senior who plans on attending a two- or four-year college you can enter to win a $1,000 scholarship. You can enter online.

378.

Win free meals
Most restaurants offer some type of free meal giveaway. Look for a fishbowl near the cash register. Drop in your business card to enter. You can print your own business cards and carry them with you wherever

How do I enter scholarship drawings?

Ready to win? Each contest has its own procedures for entering. Most allow you to enter by signing up on their website. SuperCollege, for example, has a simple application form that takes about a minute to complete. You can enter to win at http://www.supercollege.com.

you dine. While you usually win a free meal, one student we know actually won a free pizza each week for a year. Not too shabby.

Guaranteed Scholarships

Guaranteed Scholarships Do Exist

We have often warned students and parents that there is no such thing as a guaranteed scholarship. Scholarships are competitions, which you win based on the quality of your application. However, there is one class of scholarships that are virtually guaranteed. These awards are usually based on some object criteria such as your grades or test scores. If you achieve certain standards, you will receive the scholarship–guaranteed.

The majority of guaranteed awards are sponsored by colleges and state governments. It is important that you carefully research your current college or colleges that you are applying to as well as your state to see if they offer any type of guaranteed award.

The following are some examples of guaranteed scholarships. Believe it or not, an amazingly high number of students don't take advantage of guaranteed scholarships simply because they didn't know they existed. After reading this chapter we're sure that you won't make this costly mistake!

379.

National Merit Scholarships

The PSAT can be one of the most lucrative tests you'll ever take. The National Merit program (http://www.nationalmerit.org), administered by the National Merit Scholarship Corporation, a non-profit organization, receives the scores for all high school juniors who take the PSAT. Using these scores they select the highest-scoring students to be named National Merit Semifinalists. About 16,000 students out of the more than 1.2 million students who take the PSAT become Semifinalists.

This alone is an honor because it means that out of all of the juniors who took the PSAT exam you are among the top scoring. Unfortunately you don't automatically win a scholarship yet. However, if you are a National Merit Semifinalist you are invited to compete for a *National Merit Scholarship*. From the 16,000 Semifinalists about 8,000 win a National Merit Scholarship that might be one of the following:

- $2,500 from the *National Merit Scholarships*
- Corporate-sponsored *Merit Scholarship* awards
- College-sponsored *Merit Scholarship* awards

The key to being honored as a National Merit Semifinalist and thus being able to compete for some money is to take the PSAT exam during your junior year. You can learn more about the PSAT including the testing dates at http://www.collegeboard.com.

380.

Automatic scholarships based on your GPA and test scores

As your parents have probably told you since birth, there's a reason to get good grades. One of those reasons is to get a scholarship from a college that automatically gives money to students with certain scores. Such guaranteed awards are based on SAT or ACT scores or GPA.

For example, Texas Tech University (http://www.ttu.edu) offers *Presidential Scholarships* for first-time freshmen that provide one-half of tuition. The award is guaranteed for students who are admitted by April 15 and who meet test score and class rank criteria.

Other schools have created a tiered system for awarding guaranteed scholarships. Wilmington College of Ohio (http://www.wilmington. edu) offers guaranteed scholarships to all incoming students who meet the following criteria:

- Up to $10,500 for students with a 2.5-4.0 GPA and an ACT score of 17-36 or minimum SAT score of 900
- Up to $12,500 for students with a 3.0-4.0 GPA and an ACT score of 18-36 or SAT score of 940 or higher

Freshmen who apply to the State University of New York at Potsdam (http://www.potsdam.edu) can receive money through the *Freshman Scholars Program* with a minimum GPA of 88 or SAT score of 1100 or ACT score of 24. The awards start at $1,000. Plus, if you maintain a 3.25 GPA while at SUNY you get this amount each year.

Take a look at your school or the schools you are interested in and see if they offer similar guaranteed scholarships. You'll probably find that many colleges offer such incentives to attract students.

381.

Scholarships for transfer students

If you find that your college is not the right fit for you, transferring may be the answer. Unfortunately, your financial aid package does not automatically transfer from one college to another. In fact, this is something you will need to factor in when considering transferring. Some colleges make the transition easier by giving you a guaranteed transfer scholarship.

For example, Ursuline College in Pepper Pike, Ohio (http://www.ursuline.edu), offers the *Ursuline Full-Time Transfer Scholarships* and *Part-Time Transfer Scholarships* for students who have at least a 3.0 college GPA. The scholarships are up to $10,000 and renewable.

If you are thinking about transferring, speak with the admission office at the colleges you are considering. Ask them what kind of financial aid package you may expect and inquire about transfer scholarships that you may be eligible to receive.

382.

You might be entitled to a state entitlement award

All states have financial aid programs for their residents. Some of these programs effectively reward students who perform at a specific academic level in high school. California, for example, has the CalGrant program that automatically gives money to the top students at each high school to attend a college in the state. Ironically, one of the biggest problems with the program is that many students aren't aware that they are eligible for a CalGrant and don't claim their money.

Many states offer similar entitlement awards. Some are based on academic merit while others on financial need. Awards may be designated for high school seniors, adult students or students in certain fields like nursing, medicine or education. Be aware that some require you to use the money only at colleges within your state.

Take a look at Chapter 11 for a list of the state agencies that manage scholarships. Contact your agency to make sure you are not leaving any money on the table.

383.

Get in-state tuition even if you're an out-of-state student

Getting in-state tuition at a public university can save you thousands of dollars. Take a look at the difference in tuition for the University of California at Berkeley. If you are not a resident of California you will have to pay an additional non-resident fee of $28,992 per year.

If you are an out-of-state student you will need to pay out-of-state tuition until you can establish state residency. This is easier in some states than others. Texas, for example, does not like students who move to their state just to use their fine educational system and then leave. One of the residency requirements is that you live in Texas for 12 months without attending a secondary institution. This makes it impossible for any student who goes directly to college in Texas from high school to gain residency. But then again the state motto is: Don't mess with Texas.

The University of California system, on the other hand, makes it possible but not easy. To become a resident you need to show three things:

> **I received a letter from a scholarship service that said if I paid a fee I was "guaranteed" to win a scholarship. Is this a scam?**
>
> Yes! With the exception of the scholarships described in this chapter, if you encounter a so-called "guaranteed" scholarship it is not a legitimate award. Scholarships are competitions and therefore no one can predict or guarantee that you will win. If you come across an offer for a guaranteed scholarship turn the other way and run!

Physical presence. You must have proof that you remained in the state for more than one year. This means not going home for the summer. You actually have to physically be in the state and be able to prove it.

Intent. You must establish ties to the state of California that show you intend to make California your home. This requires giving up any previous residence and getting proof such as a California driver's license.

Financial independence. If both of your parents are non-residents, you must show that you are financially independent. You qualify if you are at least 24 years old, are a veteran of the U.S. Armed Forces, are a ward of the court or both parents are deceased, have legal dependents besides a spouse, are married or are a single student and have not been claimed as an income tax deduction by your parents for the past year for graduate students or past two years for undergraduate students.

California's rules are fairly common among the states. If you are planning to attend a public college outside of your own state, contact the admission office and make sure you understand what you need to do to get state residency. Once you do you'll save a bundle, and it's just like winning a guaranteed scholarship.

384.

Take advantage of residency discount agreements

Some schools have formed relationships with neighboring states to offer their residents automatic in-state rates from the beginning. The University of Arkansas, for example, offers a *Non-Resident Tuition Award* for entering freshmen from neighboring states that include Texas, Mississippi, Louisiana, Kansas, Missouri, Oklahoma and Tennessee. You must meet the minimum academic criteria of a 3.3 GPA or higher and an ACT score of at least 24 or an SAT score of at least 1160. If you meet these academic qualifications and are from a neighboring state you will be granted in-state tuition, which can save you up to $16,000 a year in fees. If you want to attend a state college in a neighboring state make sure you contact the admission office to find out if any such discount agreements are in effect.

FIVE

Reward Programs For Students

Save Money By Spending Money

You're probably familiar with airline frequent flyer programs. The idea is simple: You earn frequent flyer miles that you eventually redeem for a free ticket. It's a nice benefit for when you'd fly anyway. It's also good for the airlines since you'll stick with one company as you build up your miles.

Some enterprising companies have brought this concept to college savings. You can earn money for college not by flying but by shopping. These companies rebate a percentage of your purchases from participating retailers into college savings plans. (See Chapter 6 for a description of various savings plans.)

The rebates range from 1 percent to more than 30 percent depending on what you purchase, and most programs allow you to get your family and friends involved. Everybody can then start to contribute to one person's educational savings. These programs offer a nice supplement to your savings, and over time you can rack up a nice chunk of change.

Since all of these student reward programs work in a similar way, look for the one that offers you the best selection of participating retailers and merchants as well as the highest rebate on the purchases you make most. Also keep in mind that these programs are relatively new and are continuously adding merchants so be sure to check their websites for the most current list of participating stores.

Some also offer branded credit cards that allow you to earn rebates on every purchase you make using the card.

385.

Upromise

Upromise is a free service in which companies give you money back for college as a way to earn your loyalty. You can designate your own child, a friend's child, a grandchild, a child you expect to have one day or yourself as the recipient of the reward program. You can change the recipient at any time and enroll relatives and friends to help save for your or your child's education.

After you join Upromise you will need to register your credit or debit cards. As you shop at participating stores a percentage from each purchase is credited to your account, which will be invested in a tax-free 529 Savings Plan. The Upromise system is easy to use since once you register your credit cards you just shop normally and your rewards are automatically credited to your savings plan.

Currently, Upromise has more than 40,000 retail stores and services participating in the program. Visit the Upromise website to get a complete list of participating retail stores and restaurants along with the rebate rates.

Website: http://www.upromise.com

What's the best way to use these reward programs?

As with any savings strategy, time is your ally. The earlier you start the better. If you begin these programs 5, 10 or even 15 years before you need the money then you give them a chance to accumulate. The other important key is to multiply your contributions by recruiting as many friends and family members as possible. The more people who contribute their rebates to your account the better. Hit up all of your relatives and friends who don't have college tuition bills headed their way.

386.

Fidelity Rewards Visa Card

If your parents are planning to use a credit card anyway, you might as well get rewards for it. With this credit card, which has no annual fee, two percent of all of your purchases may be contributed to your 529 plan. Grandparents or other relatives can also get the card and contribute their rewards to your 529 plan. As you might expect, the catch is that it must be a Fidelity 529 plan. So it's important to figure out if Fidelity has the right plan for you. The investment firm offers four plans that are available to all U.S. residents.

Website: http://www.fidelity.com

387.

SAGE Scholars Tuition Rewards

When you invest with one of the program's partners, you earn tuition reward points each year. As the program describes, "Tuition reward points are like frequent flyer miles—but for college tuition." The points may be redeemed at one of almost 400 participating private colleges and universities across the country. Each point is worth $1 in scholarships at the participating institutions, and students may use the points to pay for up to 25 percent of the cost of tuition. There is a list of partner programs that you may invest in on the website, and

---

Can I rely on reward programs to pay for all of my education?

Unless you are the shopper of the century, the short answer is: no. While these programs are a nice enhancement to your overall savings strategy you should not rely on them alone to generate the money you need for college. Think of these programs as one of many tools that you'll use to build your savings future.

it includes the Pennsylvania 529 College Savings Program as well as banks and credit unions.

Website: http://www.tuitionrewards.com

Save For College

Saving For College

College is an investment in your future. With few exceptions, you are going to have to contribute some of your own money to pay for it. Even though we won a lot of scholarships—more than $100,000 between the two of us—we still had to fork over some of our own money to pay for our tuition. While it is always better to get free cash from scholarships and financial aid, the reality is that the more you save the more options you'll have.

Your personal savings is your best ally when it comes to paying for college. Scholarships will always be competitions with no guarantees that you'll win. Financial aid changes each year depending on the budgets of the government and college. There is no guarantee, even if you deserve it, that you will receive all of the financial aid that you need to pay for school.

Plus, if you were planning to take out a student loan (and most students do borrow some amount to pay for school) your savings will multiply in value. For example, let's say you end up borrowing $50,000 to pay for all four years of college. At 5.05 percent interest over 10 years (the typical term for a student loan) you would end up paying more than $13,786 in interest. But if you were able to save half of that amount and borrowed only $25,000 you would pay only $6,893 in interest. That means your personal savings just helped you to avoid $6,893 in additional interest payments.

There is one last benefit of your savings. Since it is your or your family's hard-earned money, it puts a real value on the price of your education. When we were at Harvard we met students from a variety of backgrounds. For some their parents had so much money that Harvard tuition was a drop in the bucket. For others it seemed like the family had to mortgage everything they owned just to pay for it. Can you guess which students worked harder? The students who felt the enormity of the price of their educations worked much harder and achieved much more than those whose educations were handed to them on a silver platter. This may not seem like much of a consolation now when you are eating Cup-O-Noodles in order to cut expenses, but trust us it does pay off in the long run.

The bottom line is that *your* savings is *your* money. You have total freedom to use it at whichever college you want. Nothing is as flexible as your own money. In this chapter we're going to show you some of the best strategies for building your savings.

Important: Before we begin remember that this information is meant to provide general guidance about your saving options. You should always check with an accountant regarding your individual situation and to make sure that tax laws haven't changed.

The Coverdell Education Savings Account

388.

Grow your money tax-free with the Coverdell Education Savings Account

Saving your money is a good thing, but it's even better when you let your money grow without having to pay the tax collector. This is a benefit of the Coverdell Education Savings Account (ESA). Once you set up the account and name a beneficiary (who must be under the age of 18) you can start contributing up to $2,000 per year to the account under current law to invest in any combination of stocks, bonds, mutual funds, certificates of deposit, money market funds and just plain cash.

As your money grows you are allowed to defer paying federal income taxes. In many states you will not have to pay state taxes either. When you are ready to use the money to pay for the beneficiary's educational expenses, which can include tuition, room and board, books and supplies, computers and transportation, you can withdraw the money tax-free.

The definition of what counts as educational expenses is quite broad for the Coverdell. In fact, your Coverdell savings is not limited to paying for college expenses, but you can also use it to pay for educational expenses for elementary and high school. This can be useful if you think you might need it to pay for private school tuition.

The big disadvantage of the Coverdell is the limits on who can contribute and how much you can contribute each year. You can contribute up to $2,000 a year per child. If you only have a year or two before your child goes to college you're not going to be able to realize a lot of tax-free gains.

Also, to be able to contribute the $2,000 per year maximum you must have a modified adjusted gross income (which is known as MAGI and you'll hear this term a lot) of $95,000 or less if you are a single tax filer or $190,000 or less if you are married and file jointly. If you make more, the amounts of your contributions are gradually reduced. If you earned more than $110,000 as a single filer or $220,000 as a joint filer you cannot contribute to a Coverdell account.

In what could be a positive or a negative depending on your investing skills, the Coverdell requires that you decide how your money is allocated. You'll actually need to pick individual investments. This can be good if you like to trade or bad if you are not comfortable making investment decisions.

Like all special savings plans with tax benefits, if you don't use the money for qualified educational expenses you will have to pay the taxes that you would otherwise owe along with a stiff 10 percent penalty. If for some reason the beneficiary of a Coverdell account does not go to college or use the money for qualified educational expenses by the age of 30, he or she can transfer it to another relative or a member of the family to avoid the penalty.

389.

Opening a Coverdell is as easy as 1-2-3

Banks, brokerage houses, securities firms and mutual fund companies offer Coverdell Education Savings Accounts. While researching where

How do I figure out my modified adjusted gross income (MAGI) to see if I qualify to contribute to a Coverdell ESA?

The Coverdell Education Savings Account as well as all of the various tax breaks for education require that you fall within a certain modified adjusted gross income (MAGI). For most taxpayers, MAGI is simply your adjusted gross income (AGI) from your 1040 tax forms. If you file your taxes using form 1040 then your MAGI is the AGI on line 37 and is modified by adding any foreign earned income exclusion, foreign housing exclusion, exclusion of income for residents of American Samoa and exclusion of income from Puerto Rico. If you file form 1040A then your MAGI is the AGI on line 21.

to open your Coverdell, be sure to note any minimums on the account. Some require that you invest a minimum amount each year to avoid paying an account maintenance fee. Also, be sure to understand the fees and commissions of each institution. Once you open an account, you will choose how your money is invested. Here are some places where you can open a Coverdell:

390. Buffalo Funds
http://www.buffalofunds.com

391. Charles Schwab
http://www.schwab.com

392. E-Trade Financial
http://www.etrade.com

393. Franklin Templeton Investments
http://www.franklintempleton.com

394. Janus Henderson Investors
https://en-us.janushenderson.com

395. Oakmark Funds
http://www.oakmark.com

396. Saturna
http://www.saturna.com

397. T.D. Ameritrade
http://www.tdameritrade.com

398. Thrivent Mutual Funds
http://www.thriventfunds.com

399. TIAA-CREF
http://www.tiaa.org

400. Wells Fargo
http://www.wellsfargo.com

401.

You can contribute to a Coverdell even if you are over the income limit

If you exceed the income limits of the Coverdell ESA you can still take advantage of the Coverdell by gifting the $2,000 to your child and having him or her open the account. This is also a way for relatives to contribute to your son or daughter's Coverdell. Remember that the total amount that your child can contribute to a Coverdell (regardless of where the money comes from) is $2,000 per year.

402.

Read exciting Coverdell examples by downloading IRS Publication 970

You can download the nitty-gritty details on the Coverdell (as well as 529 Plans and other tax breaks) by getting the latest version of IRS

Publication 970. Visit http://www.irs.gov, and search for "Publication 970" on the front page.

While the document is typical of most IRS publications, one nice feature is the examples. Here is one reprinted from the section on the Coverdell, which explains how the contribution limits work when several relatives set up a Coverdell to benefit a single child.

When Maria Luna was born in 2018, three separate Coverdell ESAs were set up for her, one by her parents, one by her grandfather and one by her aunt. In 2019, the total of all contributions to Maria's three Coverdell ESAs cannot be more than $2,000. For example, if her grandfather contributed $2,000 to one of her Coverdell ESAs, no one else could contribute to any of her three accounts. Or, if her parents contributed $1,000 and her aunt $600, her grandfather or someone else could contribute no more than $400. These contributions could be put into any of Maria's Coverdell ESA accounts.

The example goes on and changes the scenario by adding another child to Maria Luna's family. *The facts are the same as in the previous example except that Maria Luna's older brother, Edgar, also has a Coverdell ESA. If their grandfather contributed $2,000 to Maria's Coverdell ESA in 2019, he could also contribute $2,000 to Edgar's Coverdell ESA.*

While IRS publications are far from pleasure reading, the examples they provide help in understanding how the rules apply in the real world.

The 529 Savings Plan

Given the buzz about the 529 Savings Plan, you'd think it was the best thing to come along since the invention of compound interest in helping you pay for college. While there are some real advantages to 529 Savings Plans, they are not magical solutions.

Like any investment, 529 Savings Plans (officially known as qualified tuition programs or QTPs), don't guarantee specific returns and rise and fall with the market. The tax-free benefits, which are really the major benefits of the plan, only apply to the earnings that are generated. This means if you only have a year or two before your child enters college you probably won't notice much of a benefit. But for long-term savings, the right 529 Savings Plan (don't worry we'll show you what to look for when selecting a plan) should help you build your college fund faster. There is also an interesting estate planning benefit to a 529 Savings Plan that your family might be able to take advantage of.

Let's take a look at the much-ballyhooed 529 Savings Plans.

403.

Grow your money tax-free with the 529 Savings Plan

The 529 Savings Plans are the toast of the town among many financial advisors. They are popular not because they have had phenomenal rates of return (many plans lose value during a down stock market) but because they allow families to stock away a lot of money tax-free. Contribution limits are much higher than the Coverdell with some plans capping the contribution at more than $500,000 per student. Plus, there are no income limits to who can contribute to a 529 Plan, which means that every family member can participate including rich Uncle Leo.

529 Savings Plans are offered by every state and the District of Columbia, and many states offer more than one plan. You don't have to participate in your own state's plan and are free to sign up for any of the 529 Plans that are out there. However, you should check your state's tax regulations since some states allow you to take a state tax deduction on the money you put into a 529 Plan. If you live in one of these states you'll probably find that with these tax savings your state plan will offer you the best deal.

All of the money that you put into your 529 Plan will grow free from federal income tax and depending on your state may also be free from state taxes as long as you use the money for qualified college educational expenses.

Unlike the Coverdell, all of the money that you put into a 529 Plan must be used for college-related expenses or else you not only pay the taxes that you would have owed on any gains but also a stiff 10 percent penalty. Fortunately, 529 Plans are very flexible when it comes to changing the beneficiary since unlike the Coverdell the money stays in your control. Even if you opened a 529 Plan for one child you don't have to use that money for that child. You can use the money from your 529 Plan for any member of your family including yourself.

So far everything about the 529 Plan sounds good. What about the downside? The disadvantage of the 529 is that your investments are determined by the plan. In other words, you don't manage which specific stocks your money is invested in. Most 529 Plans have different investment tracks such as conservative, moderate and aggressive. In addition, most offer an age-based option that is more aggressive when

---

How much will a four-year public college cost when my child graduates from high school?

According to the College Board the average one-year cost for tuition and room and board at a four-year public college is $19,080. Assuming a 7 percent increase in costs each year you can use this table to project what the average total cost will be when your child heads off to school.

Years until student begins college	Total estimated cost of a four-year public education
1	$90,644
2	$96,989
3	$103,778
4	$111,043
5	$118,816
7	$136,032
10	$166,645
12	$190,792
15	$233,729

your child is younger and becomes increasingly conservative as your child gets closer to college age. In this sense a 529 Savings Plan is like a mutual fund where you rely on the fund manager to pick the right mix of investments. But unlike stocks or mutual funds, once you've chosen a track for your 529 Plan, you usually can't modify it for a year. You can also change between different 529 Plans only once a year.

Like any investment, 529 Savings Plans are tied to the market. When the market is good, 529 Savings Plans generally rise in value. When the market is bad, 529 Savings Plans generally fall. Fortunately, with many that offer an age-based program as your child nears high school graduation the funds shift more of your money out of volatile investments and into safer bonds and cash.

It's important to remember that 529 Savings Plans are not a quick fix to your college money needs. To make a 529 Savings Plan work you need to be a consistent saver over a long period of time. You also need good returns on your money since the primary benefit is not having to pay taxes on the gains.

404.

What to consider when choosing a 529 Savings Plan

Since you can participate in any state's 529 Savings Plan regardless of where you live, you have many options. Maybe too many. When you are considering the merits of each plan focus on these areas before you invest:

Low expense ratio and other fees. Know what all of the fees are before you sign up. Pay particular attention to annual account maintenance fees, transfer fees and commissions. The annual account maintenance fee is a percentage and is also known as the expense ratio. We recommend that you try to find a plan that has an expense ratio that is under 1 percent a year.

State benefits. You may be eligible for significant benefits if you invest in your own state's plan. These benefits may include state tax deductions on contributions and/or earnings and can more than make up for other shortcomings of the plan. A few states even offer matching contributions!

Investment track options. More options are usually better. Look for a plan that gives you a good mix of investment tracks. (Remember you can usually switch tracks only once a year.) You want as much flexibility in your plan as possible.

Ease of changing account beneficiary. Make sure you can change the beneficiary in case your child does not need all of the money for college.

Other less important considerations include the minimum amount you need to open the account, conveniences such as online transactions and whether or not the plan accepts contributions at any time in the year.

405.

Beware of the pitfall of 529 Savings Plans

One of the dangers of all 529 Savings Plans is that because the plans are relatively new the rules are still changing. Here is one dangerous trend that you need to be aware of before investing:

A few states have begun to charge a tax on the earnings of 529 Plans sponsored by other states. If you live in one of these states it effectively makes most out-of-state 529 Plans very unattractive. As state budgets shrink you can expect more states to do this to generate additional revenue.

406.

If you live in a state that allows a deduction, take it

If you live in one of the following states your 529 Plans may allow a state tax deduction or credit for contributions to your 529 Plan. This is a huge benefit that you should consider when examining your state's own 529 Plan. Remember that tax laws can change so check with your state tax office or accountant to verify that you can still deduct contributions to your 529 Plans. Also, some states place limits on the maximum amount that can be deducted in one year.

- Alabama
- Arizona
- Arkansas
- Colorado
- Connecticut
- District of Columbia
- Georgia
- Idaho
- Illinois
- Indiana
- Iowa
- Kansas
- Louisiana
- Maine
- Maryland
- Massachusetts
- Michigan
- Minnesota
- Mississippi
- Missouri
- Montana
- Nebraska
- New Mexico
- New York
- North Dakota
- Ohio
- Oklahoma
- Oregon
- Pennsylvania
- Rhode Island
- South Carolina
- Utah
- Vermont
- Virginia
- West Virginia
- Wisconsin

Prepaid College Tuition Plans

407.

Pre-pay your education with the Prepaid Tuition Plan

Prepaid College Tuition Plans are the first cousins of 529 Plans. These plans are run by your state's Treasurer's Office and allow you to contribute a fixed amount of money on a monthly or yearly basis to buy a fixed number of tuition credits at a public college or university at today's prices. This effectively allows you to pre-pay for your child's tuition.

If prices go up (and you can bet that they will) by the time your child is ready to enter college the prepaid program will cover any increase. Most prepaid plans require that your child be a high school freshman or younger when you start the plan. These plans are good if you think your child will attend your state's college or university. The risk is that

---

How much will a four-year private college cost when my child graduates from high school?

According to the College Board the average one-year cost for tuition and room and board at a four-year private college is $46,680. Assuming a 7 percent increase in costs each year you can use this table to project what the average total cost will be when your child heads off to school.

Years until student begins college	Total estimated cost of a 4-year private education
1	$221,764
2	$237,288
3	$253,898
4	$271,671
5	$290,688
7	$332,809
10	$407,705
12	$466,781
15	$571,827

your child will want to attend a private college or out-of-state school. In this case you will usually be refunded what you put into the plan along with some interest. Since private or out-of-state public schools often cost more than in-state schools, the amount you get back is usually not enough to pay for the more expensive choice of your child.

It is very important to understand what you are buying with a prepaid plan. Some states' prepaid plans cover tuition but not room and board, which can be a hefty expense. Be sure you also understand what happens if your child decides not to go to that school and if you are able to change beneficiaries.

Your State's 529 And Prepaid Tuition Plans

You don't need to join your state's 529 Savings Plan, and you are free to sign up for any state's plan. Just be sure that you know what state benefits, if any, you may miss by not using your state's plan.

Some states also offer more than one 529 Savings Plan. Most states contract the management of their 529 Plans to investment companies like TIAA-CREF or Fidelity. A good resource to get an overview of all of the state's plans can be found at the College Savings Plans Network at http://www.collegesavings.org. Here is an overview of each state's plan:

408. Alabama

Savings Plans

> Fund: CollegeCounts 529 Fund
> Administrator: Union Bank & Trust Company
> State tax deduction for contributions: Yes
> State allows tax-free withdrawals: Yes
> Website: http://www.collegecounts529.com
> Phone: 866-529-2228

> Fund: Enable Savings Plan Alabama
> Administrator: Nebraska State Treasurer
> State tax deduction for contributions: No
> State allows tax-free withdrawals: Yes

Website: https://al.enablesavings.com
Phone: 866-833-7949

409. Alaska

Savings Plans

Fund: University of Alaska College Savings Plan
Administrator: T. Rowe Price
State tax deduction for contributions: No state income tax
State allows tax-free withdrawals: No state income tax
Website: http://www.uacollegesavings.com
Phone: 866-277-1005

Fund: T. Rowe Price College Savings Plan
Administrator: T. Rowe Price
State tax deduction for contributions: No state income tax
State allows tax-free withdrawals: No state income tax
Website: http://www.price529.com
Phone: 800-369-3641

Fund: John Hancock Freedom 529
Administrator: John Hancock
State tax deduction for contributions: No state income tax
State allows tax-free withdrawals: No state income tax
Website: http://www.jhinvestments.com/College/Overview.
aspx
Phone: 866-222-7498

Prepaid Tuition Plan

The University of Alaska College Savings Plan offers as one of
its portfolio choices the Advanced College Tuition (ACT) track
that allows you to lock in the cost of tuition for the University
of Alaska at today's prices.

410. Arizona

Savings Plans

Fund: Arizona Family College Savings Program
Administrator: College Savings Bank

State tax deduction for contributions: Yes
State allows tax-free withdrawals: Yes
Website: http://az529.gov
Phone: 800-888-2723

Fund: Fidelity Arizona College Savings Plan
Administrator: Fidelity Investments
State tax deduction for contributions: Yes
State allows tax-free withdrawals: Yes
Website: https://www.fidelity.com/529-plans/arizona
Phone: 800-544-1262

Fund: Ivy InvestEd 529 Plan
Administrator: Ivy Investment Management Company
State tax deduction for contributions: Yes
State allows tax-free withdrawals: Yes
Website: http://www.ivyinvestments.com/products/ivy-invested-529-plan
Phone: 800-877-6472

411. Arkansas

Savings Plan

Fund: GIFT College Investing Plan
Administrator: Ascensus College Savings
State tax deduction for contributions: Yes
State allows tax-free withdrawals: Yes
Website: http://www.thegiftplan.com
Phone: 800-587-7301

Fund: iShares 529 Plan
Administrator: Ascensus Broker Dealer Services Inc.
State tax deduction for contributions: Yes
State allows tax-free withdrawals: Yes
Website: http://www.ishares529.com
Phone: 888-529-9552

412. California

Savings Plan

Fund: ScholarShare College Savings Plan
Administrator: TIAA-CREF Tuition Financing Inc.
State tax deduction for contributions: No
State allows tax-free withdrawals: Yes
Website: http://www.scholarshare.com
Phone: 800-544-5248

413. Colorado

Savings Plans

Fund: Direct Portfolio College Savings Plan
Administrator: Ascensus Broker Dealer Services Inc. and The
Vanguard Group, Inc.
State tax deduction for contributions: Yes
State allows tax-free withdrawals: Yes
Website: http://www.collegeinvest.org
Phone: 800-997-4295

Fund: Scholars Choice College Savings Program
Administrator: Legg Mason Inc.
State tax deduction for contributions: Yes
State allows tax-free withdrawals: Yes
Website: http://www.scholars-choice.com
Phone: 888-572-4652

Fund: Stable Value Plus College Savings Program
Administrator: MetLife
State tax deduction for contributions: Yes
State allows tax-free withdrawals: Yes
Website: http://www.collegeinvest.org
Phone: 800-478-5651

Fund: Smart Choice College Savings Plan
Administrator: FirstBank Holding Company
State tax deduction for contributions: Yes
State allows tax-free withdrawals: Yes

Website: http://www.collegeinvest.org
Phone: 800-964-3444

414. Connecticut

Savings Plan

Fund: Connecticut Higher Education Trust
Administrator: TIAA-CREF Tuition Financing Inc.
State tax deduction for contributions: Yes
State allows tax-free withdrawals: Yes
Website: http://www.aboutchet.com
Phone: 888-799-2438

415. Delaware

Savings Plan

Fund: Delaware College Investment Plan
Administrator: Fidelity Investments
State tax deduction for contributions: No
State allows tax-free withdrawals: Yes
Website: https://www.fidelity.com/529-plans/delaware
Phone: 800-544-1655

416. District of Columbia

Savings Plan

Fund: DC 529 College Savings Program
Administrator: Ascensus College Savings
State tax deduction for contributions: Yes
State allows tax-free withdrawals: Yes
Website: http://www.dccollegesavings.com
Phone: 800-987-4859

417. Florida

Savings Plan

Fund: Florida 529 Savings Plan
Administrator: Florida Prepaid College Board
State tax deduction for contributions: No state income tax
State allows tax-free withdrawals: No state income tax
Website: http://www.myfloridaprepaid.com
Phone: 800-552-4723

Prepaid Tuition Plan

Fund: Florida Prepaid College Plan
Administrator: Florida Prepaid College Board
State tax deduction for contributions: No state income tax
State allows tax-free withdrawals: No state income tax
Website: http://www.myfloridaprepaid.com
Phone: 800-552-4723

418. Georgia

Savings Plan

Fund: Path2College 529 Plan
Administrator: TIAA-CREF Tuition Financing Inc.
State tax deduction for contributions: Yes
State allows tax-free withdrawals: Yes
Website: http://www.path2college529.com
Phone: 877-424-4377

419. Hawaii

Savings Plan

Fund: Hawaii's College Savings Program
Administrator: Ascensus College Savings and The Vanguard
Group
State tax deduction for contributions: No
State allows tax-free withdrawals: Yes

Website: http://www.hi529.com
Phone: 866-529-3343

420. Idaho

Savings Plan

Fund: Idaho College Savings Program/IDeal
Administrator: Ascensus College Savings
State tax deduction for contributions: Yes
State allows tax-free withdrawals: Yes
Website: http://www.idsaves.org
Phone: 866-433-2533

421. Illinois

Savings Plan

Fund: Bright Start College Savings Program
Administrator: Union Bank & Trust Company
State tax deduction for contributions: Yes
State allows tax-free withdrawals: Yes
Website: http://www.brightstartsavings.com
Phone: 877-432-7444

Fund: Bright Directions College Savings Program
Administrator: Northern Trust Securities
State tax deduction for contributions: Yes
State allows tax-free withdrawals: Yes
Website: http://www.brightdirections.com
Phone: 866-722-7283

Prepaid Tuition Plan

Fund: College Illinois!
Administrator: Illinois Student Assistance Commission
State tax deduction for contributions: Yes
State allows tax-free withdrawals: Yes
Website: http://www.collegeillinois.org
Phone: 877-877-3724

422. Indiana

Savings Plan

Fund: CollegeChoice 529 Direct Savings Plan
Administrator: Ascensus College Savings
State tax deduction for contributions: Yes
State allows tax-free withdrawals: Yes
Website: https://www.collegechoicedirect.com
Phone: 866-485-9415

Fund: CollegeChoice CD 529 Direct Savings Plan
Administrator: College Savings Bank
State tax deduction for contributions: Yes
State allows tax-free withdrawals: Yes
Website: http://www.collegechoicecd.com
Phone: 888-913-2885

423. Iowa

Savings Plan

Fund: College Savings Iowa
Administrator: State Treasurer of Iowa, Ascensus College
Savings and Vanguard
State tax deduction for contributions: Yes
State allows tax-free withdrawals: Yes
Website: https://www.collegesavingsiowa.com
Phone: 888-672-9116

Fund: IAdvisor 529 Plan
Administrator: Voya Investment Management Co. LLC
State tax deduction for contributions: Yes
State allows tax-free withdrawals: Yes
Website: http://www.iowaadvisor529.com
Phone: 800-774-5127

424. Kansas

Savings Plan

Fund: Schwab 529 College Savings Plan
Administrator: Charles Schwab and American Century
State tax deduction for contributions: Yes
State allows tax-free withdrawals: Yes
Website: http://www.schwab.com/529
Phone: 866-903-3863

Fund: Learning Quest Education Savings Program
Administrator: American Century
State tax deduction for contributions: Yes
State allows tax-free withdrawals: Yes
Website: http://www.learningquest.com
Phone: 800-579-2203

425. Kentucky

Savings Plan

Fund: Kentucky Education Savings Plan Trust
Administrator: TIAA-CREF
State tax deduction for contributions: No
State allows tax-free withdrawals: Yes
Website: http://www.kysaves.com
Phone: 877-598-7878

426. Louisiana

Savings Plan

Fund: START Saving Program
Administrator: Louisiana State Treasurer
State tax deduction for contributions: Yes
State allows tax-free withdrawals: Yes
Website: http://www.startsaving.la.gov
Phone: 800-259-5626, ext. 1012

427. Maine

Savings Plan

Fund: NextGen College Investing Plan
Administrator: Merrill Lynch, Pierce, Fenner & Smith Inc.
State tax deduction for contributions: No
State allows tax-free withdrawals: Yes
Website: http://www.nextgenforme.com
Phone: 877-463-9843

428. Maryland

Savings Plan

Fund: Maryland College Investment Plan
Administrator: T. Rowe Price
State tax deduction for contributions: Yes
State allows tax-free withdrawals: Yes
Website: http://www.maryland529.com
Phone: 888-463-4723

Prepaid Tuition Plan

Fund: Maryland Prepaid College Trust
Administrator: State
State tax deduction for contributions: Yes
State allows tax-free withdrawals: Yes
Website: http://www.maryland529.com
Phone: 888-463-4723

429. Massachusetts

Savings Plan

Fund: U.Fund College Investing Plan
Administrator: Fidelity Investments
State tax deduction for contributions: Yes (2017-2021)
State allows tax-free withdrawals: Yes
Website: https://www.fidelity.com/529-plans/massachusetts
Phone: 800-544-2776

Prepaid Tuition Plan

Fund: U.Plan
Administrator: State
You participate in U.Plan by purchasing a special state bond. This bond is free of Massachusetts state income tax. You'll have to check with your accountant, but this state bond may also be free of federal income tax.
Website: http://www.mefa.org/uplan/
Phone: 800-449-6332

430. Michigan

Savings Plan

Fund: Michigan Education Savings Plan
Administrator: TIAA-CREF
State tax deduction for contributions: Yes
State allows tax-free withdrawals: Yes
Website: http://www.misaves.com
Phone: 877-861-6377

Fund: MI 529 Advisor Plan
Administrator: TIAA-CREF and Nuveen Securities
State tax deduction for contributions: Yes
State allows tax-free withdrawals: Yes
Website: http://www.mi529advisor.com
Phone: 866-529-8818

Prepaid Tuition Plan

Fund: Michigan Education Trust
Administrator: State
State tax deduction for contributions: Yes
State allows tax-free withdrawals: Yes
Website: http://www.michigan.gov/setwithmet
Phone: 800-MET-4-KID

431. Minnesota

Savings Plan

Fund: Minnesota College Savings Plan
Administrator: TIAA-CREF
State tax deduction for contributions: Yes
State allows tax-free withdrawals: Yes
Website: http://www.mnsaves.org
Phone: 877-338-4646

432. Mississippi

Savings Plan

Fund: Mississippi Affordable College Savings Program
Administrator: Intuition College Savings Solutions LLC
State tax deduction for contributions: Yes
State allows tax-free withdrawals: Yes
Website: https://access.ms529.com
Phone: 800-987-4450

Prepaid Tuition Plan

Fund: Mississippi Prepaid Affordable College Tuition Program
Administrator: State
State tax deduction for contributions: Yes
State allows tax-free withdrawals: Yes
Website: http://www.treasurerlynnfitch.ms.gov/collegesavingsmississippi/
Phone: 800-987-4450

433. Missouri

Savings Plan

Fund: MOST - Missouri's 529 College Savings Plan
Administrator: Ascensus College Savings
State tax deduction for contributions: Yes

State allows tax-free withdrawals: Yes
Website: http://www.missourimost.org
Phone: 888-414-6678

434. Montana

Savings Plans

Fund: Achieve Montana
Administrator: Ascensus College Savings and Vanguard
Group
State tax deduction for contributions: Yes
State allows tax-free withdrawals: Yes
Website: https://www.achievemontana.com
Phone: 800-888-2723

435. Nebraska

Savings Plans

Fund: Nebraska Education Savings Trust
Administrator: First National Bank of Omaha
State tax deduction for contributions: Yes
State allows tax-free withdrawals: Yes
Website: https://www.nest529direct.com
Phone: 888-993-3746

Fund: State Farm College Savings Plan
Administrator: First National Bank of Omaha
State tax deduction for contributions: Yes
State allows tax-free withdrawals: Yes
Website: http://www.statefarm.com
Phone: 800-321-7520

Fund: TD Ameritrade 529 College Savings Plan
Administrator: TD Ameritrade
State tax deduction for contributions: Yes
State allows tax-free withdrawals: Yes
Website: http://www.tdameritrade.com
Phone: 877-408-4644

436. Nevada

Savings Plans

Fund: Putnam 529 for America
Administrator: Putnam Investments
State tax deductions for contributions: No income tax
State allows tax-free withdrawals: No income tax
Website: http://www.putnam.com
Phone: 877-788-6265

Fund: USAA College Savings Plan
Administrator: USAA Investment Management
State tax deductions for contributions: No income tax
State allows tax-free withdrawals: No income tax
Website: http://www.usaa.com
Phone: 800-531-8722

Fund: SSGA Upromise 529 Plan
Administrator: Ascensus College Savings
State tax deductions for contributions: No income tax
State allows tax-free withdrawals: No income tax
Website: http://www.ssga.upromise529.com
Phone: 866-967-2776

Fund: Vanguard 529 College Savings
Administrator: Vanguard
State tax deductions for contributions: No income tax
State allows tax-free withdrawals: No income tax
Website: http://www.vanguard.com/vanguard529
Phone: 866-734-4530

Fund: Wealthfront 529 College Savings Plan
Administrator: Ascensus College Savings
State tax deductions for contributions: No income tax
State allows tax-free withdrawals: No income tax
Website: http://www.wealthfront.com/529
Phone: 650-249-4250

Prepaid Tuition Plan

Fund: Nevada Prepaid Tuition Program

Administrator: State
State tax deductions for contributions: No income tax
State allows tax-free withdrawals: No income tax
Website: https://www.nvprepaid.gov
Phone: 888-477-2667

437. New Hampshire

Savings Plans

Fund: UNIQUE College Investing
Administrator: Fidelity Investments
State tax deductions for contributions: No income tax
State allows tax-free withdrawals: No income tax
Website: https://www.fidelity.com/529-plans/new-hampshire
Phone: 800-544-1914

Fund: Fidelity Advisor 529 Plan
Administrator: Fidelity Advisor Funds
State tax deductions for contributions: No income tax
State allows tax-free withdrawals: No income tax
Website: http://institutional.fidelity.com
Phone: 877-208-0098

438. New Jersey

Savings Plans

Fund: NJBEST 529 College Savings Plan
Administrator: Franklin Templeton
State tax deductions for contributions: No
State allows tax-free withdrawals: Yes
Website: http://www.njbest.com
Phone: 877-465-2378

Fund: Franklin Templeton 529 College Savings Plan
Administrator: Franklin Templeton
State tax deductions for contributions: No
State allows tax-free withdrawals: Yes

Website: http://www.franklintempleton.com
Phone: 866-362-1597

439. New Mexico

Savings Plans

Fund: The Education Plan's College Savings Program
Administrator: Oppenheimer Funds
State tax deductions for contributions: Yes
State allows tax-free withdrawals: Yes
Website: http://www.theeducationplan.com
Phone: 877-337-5268

Fund: Scholar'sEdge
Administrator: OppenheimerFunds
State tax deductions for contributions: Yes
State allows tax-free withdrawals: Yes
Website: http://www.scholarsedge529.com
Phone: 866-529-7283

440. New York

Savings Plan

Fund: New York's College Savings Program
Administrator: Ascensus College Savings
State tax deductions for contributions: Yes
State allows tax-free withdrawals: Yes
Website: http://www.nysaves.org
Phone: 877-697-2837

Fund: New York's 529 Advisor-Guided College Savings Plan
Administrator: Ascensus
State tax deductions for contributions: Yes
State allows tax-free withdrawals: Yes
Website: http://www.ny529advisor.com
Phone: 800-774-2108

441. North Carolina

Savings Plan

Fund: National College Savings Program
Administrator: College Foundation Inc.
State tax deductions for contributions: No
State allows tax-free withdrawals: Yes
Website: http://www.nc529.org
Phone: 800-600-3453

442. North Dakota

Savings Plan

Fund: College SAVE
Administrator: Ascensus College Savings
State tax deductions for contributions: Yes
State allows tax-free withdrawals: Yes
Website: http://www.collegesave4u.com
Phone: 866-728-3529

443. Ohio

Savings Plan

Fund: Ohio CollegeAdvantage 529 Savings Plan
Administrator: Ohio Tuition Trust Authority
State tax deductions for contributions: Yes
State allows tax-free withdrawals: Yes
Website: http://www.collegeadvantage.com
Phone: 800-233-6734

Fund: BlackRock CollegeAdvantage
Administrator: BlackRock Advisors LLC
State tax deductions for contributions: Yes
State allows tax-free withdrawals: Yes

Website: http://www.blackrock.com
Phone: 866-529-8582

444. Oklahoma

Savings Plan

Fund: Oklahoma College Savings Plan
Administrator: TIAA-CREF
State tax deductions for contributions: Yes
State allows tax-free withdrawals: Yes
Website: http://www.ok4saving.org
Phone: 877-654-7284

Fund: Oklahoma Dream 529 Plan
Administrator: TIAA-Tuition Financing and Allianz Global
State tax deductions for contributions: Yes
State allows tax-free withdrawals: Yes
Website: http://www.okdream529.com
Phone: 877-529-9299

445. Oregon

Savings Plans

Fund: Oregon College Savings Plan
Administrator: Sumday Administration LLC
State tax deductions for contributions: Yes
State allows tax-free withdrawals: Yes
Website: http://www.oregoncollegesavings.com
Phone: 866-772-8464

Fund: MFS 529 Savings Plan
Administrator: MFS Fund Distributors Inc.
State tax deductions for contributions: Yes
State allows tax-free withdrawals: Yes
Website: http://www.mfs.com
Phone: 866-637-7526

446. Pennsylvania

Savings Plan

Fund: Pennsylvania 529 Investment Plan
Administrator: Pennsylvania Treasury Department
State tax deductions for contributions: Yes
State allows tax-free withdrawals: Yes
Website: http://www.pa529.com
Phone: 800-440-4000

Prepaid Tuition Plan

Fund: Pennsylvania 529 Guaranteed Savings Plan
Administrator: State
State tax deductions for contributions: Yes
State allows tax-free withdrawals: Yes
Website: http://www.pa529.com
Phone: 800-440-4000

447. Rhode Island

Savings Plans

Fund: CollegeBound Saver
Administrator: Ascensus College Savings
State tax deductions for contributions: Yes
State allows tax-free withdrawals: Yes
Website: https://www.collegeboundsaver.com
Phone: 877-517-4829

Fund: CollegeBound 529
Administrator: Ascensus with Invesco Distributors
State tax deductions for contributions: Yes
State allows tax-free withdrawals: Yes
Website: https://www.invesco.com
Phone: 877-615-4116

448. South Carolina

Savings Plan

Fund: Future Scholar 529 College Savings Plan
Administrator: Columbia Management
State tax deductions for contributions: Yes
State allows tax-free withdrawals: Yes
Website: http://www.futurescholar.com
Phone: 888-244-5674

449. South Dakota

Savings Plans

Fund: College Access 529
Administrator: Allianz Global Investors
State tax deductions for contributions: No income tax
State allows tax-free withdrawals: No income tax
Website: http://www.collegeaccess529.com
Phone: 866-529-7462

450. Tennessee

Savings Plans

Fund: TNStars College Savings 529 Plan
Administrator: State
State tax deductions for contributions: No income tax
State allows tax-free withdrawals: No income tax
Website: http://www.tnstars.com
Phone: 855-386-7827

451. Texas

Savings Plan

Fund: Lonestar 529 Plan
Administrator: NorthStar Financial Services Group LLC
State tax deductions for contributions: No income tax
State allows tax-free withdrawals: No income tax

Website: http://www.lonestar529.com
Phone: 800-445-4723

Fund: Texas College Savings Plan
Administrator: NorthStar Financial Services Group LLC
State tax deductions for contributions: No income tax
State allows tax-free withdrawals: No income tax
Website: http://www.texascollegesavings.com
Phone: 800-445-4723, option 3

Prepaid Tuition Plan

Fund: Texas Tuition Promise Fund
Administrator: State
State tax deductions for contributions: No income tax
State allows tax-free withdrawals: No income tax
Website: http://www.texastuitionpromisefund.com
Phone: 800-445-4723

452. Utah

Savings Plan

Fund: my529
Administrator: Utah Higher Education Assistance Authority
State tax deductions for contributions: Yes
State allows tax-free withdrawals: Yes
Website: http://www.my529.org
Phone: 800-418-2551

453. Vermont

Savings Plan

Fund: Vermont Higher Education Investment Plan
Administrator: Vermont Student Assistance Corp and
Intuition College Savings Solutions LLC
State tax deductions for contributions: Yes
State allows tax-free withdrawals: Yes
Website: http://www.vheip.org
Phone: 800-637-5860

454. Virginia

Savings Plans

Fund: CollegeAmerica
Administrator: American Funds
State tax deductions for contributions: Yes
State allows tax-free withdrawals: Yes
Website: http://www.americanfunds.com/college/collegeamerica.html
Phone: 800-421-4225

Fund: Virginia Invest529
Administrator: Virginia 529 Board
State tax deductions for contributions: Yes
State allows tax-free withdrawals: Yes
Website: http://www.virginia529.com
Phone: 888-567-0540

Prepaid Tuition Plan

Fund: Virginia Prepaid529
Administrator: Virginia529
State tax deductions for contributions: Yes
State allows tax-free withdrawals: Yes
Website: http://www.virginia529.com
Phone: 888-567-0540

455. Washington

Prepaid Tuition Plan

Fund: Guaranteed Education Tuition of Washington (GET)
Administrator: State
State tax deductions for contributions: No income tax
State allows tax-free withdrawals: No income tax
Website: http://www.get.wa.gov
Phone: 800-955-2318

Fund: DreamAhead College Investment Plan
Administrator: Sumday Administration, LLC
State tax deductions for contributions: No income tax
State allows tax-free withdrawals: No income tax
Website: http://www.dreamahead.wa.gov
Phone: 844-529-5845

456. West Virginia

Savings Plan

Fund: SMART529 Direct College Savings Plan
Administrator: Hartford Securities
State tax deductions for contributions: Yes
State allows tax-free withdrawals: Yes
Website: http://www.smart529.com
Phone: 866-574-3542

Fund: SMART529 Select
Administrator: Hartford Securities
State tax deductions for contributions: Yes
State allows tax-free withdrawals: Yes
Website: http://www.smart529select.com
Phone: 866-574-3542

Fund: The Hartford SMART529
Administrator: Hartford Securities
State tax deductions for contributions: Yes
State allows tax-free withdrawals: Yes
Website: http://www.hartfordfunds.com
Phone: 866-574-3542

457. Wisconsin

Savings Plans

Fund: EdVest
Administrator: TIAA-CREF Tuition Financing Inc.
State tax deductions for contributions: Yes
State allows tax-free withdrawals: Yes
Website: http://www.edvest.com
Phone: 888-338-3789

Fund: Tomorrow's Scholar
Administrator: Voya Investments Distributor LLC
State tax deductions for contributions: Yes
State allows tax-free withdrawals: Yes
Website: http://www.tomorrowsscholar.com
Phone: 866-677-6933

458. Wyoming

Savings Plan

Wyoming no longer operates a 529 savings plan.

459.

Consider transferring a custodial account to a 529 Plan

Before 529 Savings Plans were established, the Uniform Transfers to Minors Act (UTMA) or Uniform Gifts to Minors Act (UGMA) were the best way to transfer money from you or a relative to your child and pay the least amount of taxes as possible. However, with the 529 Savings Plan you pay no taxes (and may even be able take a state deduction on your contributions) as long as the money is used to pay for college.

So consider transferring the money currently in a UTMA/UGMA into a 529 Savings Plan. Most 529 Plans accept funds from a custodial account. However, 529 Plans can usually only accept cash, which means any investments in a custodial account must be liquidated and taxes paid on the gains before they can be transferred into a 529 Plan. Be sure you estimate the taxes that you might owe should you cash out a custodial account. Also, remember that the money in a UTMA/UGMA was gifted to your child and therefore will become his or her money at the age of maturity, which is either at age 18 or 21 depending on the laws in your state. Therefore, this money can only be used to pay for your child's education and cannot be switched to another beneficiary.

460.

Jump-start your 529 Savings Plan with a super gift

If you or a relative has a chunk of cash that you want to give your child or grandchild to pay for college, you are limited by the current $15,000 annual gift exclusion. This means that if you give more than $15,000 per year you will be subject to gift tax. However, with a 529 Plan you can actually make five year's worth of gifts in one year. So that means that you could give $75,000 if you are single or $150,000 as a couple to your child or grandchild and count it as a gift made over the next five years. You will not incur any gift taxes, and your beneficiary will have access to this significant sum of money. This may be an excellent way for grandparents to transfer a large part of their estate without incurring additional taxes.

461.

For private colleges consider the Private College 529 Plan

The Private College 529 Plan is a prepaid program sponsored by a consortium of almost 300 private universities and colleges. The program has the same federal tax benefits as state-sponsored 529 Plans. Under the Private College 529 Plan you purchase tuition credits at today's prices. This gives you the ability to freeze tuition at today's rate. As the cost of college increases the plan will cover the difference between what you paid for the credit and what tuition actually costs when your child is ready to attend school. As with all prepaid tuition programs the key risk is that your child may not want to attend one of the participating schools. Also, saving through the Private College 529 Plan does guarantee your child admission into any of the member schools.

We recommend that you check out the program by visiting their website and view the list of participating colleges. This is definitely an innovative twist on the traditional 529 Plan. Website: http://www. privatecollege529plan.com.

462.

Compare Coverdell ESAs, 529 Savings Plans and Prepaid Tuition Plans to pick the right one for you

So far we have discussed the Coverdell Education Savings Account, the 529 Savings Plan and the Prepaid Tuition Plan. Here is a quick summary of the major highlights and lowlights of each to help you decide what is right for you.

Coverdell ESA

■ All distributions are tax-free as long as they are used for qualified educational expenses.

■ You have total control over how your money is invested. You can choose which stocks, bonds or mutual fund to invest your money in or you can hold your money in cash.

■ You can use your money to pay for primary and secondary educational expenses including tuition, room, board, uniforms, tutoring and even computer equipment and software.

■ Coverdell accounts may be owned by the student or the student's parent. Under the Federal methodology which is used by most public universities to determine eligibility for financial aid, Coverdell accounts are considered the asset of the parent which means it will have a small impact on the student's chances of receiving financial aid.

■ The money must be used by the beneficiary or designated to another relative before the beneficiary turns 30.

■ The annual contribution limit is $2,000 per beneficiary, which means you have to start early to make the Coverdell effective.

■ There are income limits on who can contribute to a Coverdell.

529 Savings Plans

■ All distributions are tax-free as long as they are used for qualified college expenses.

■ The funds in the plan are controlled by the contributor. This means that parents can make sure the money is used for college and can also transfer it to another beneficiary if necessary.

■ The contribution limits are very high.

■ There is no income limitation to who can contribute money to a 529 Savings Plan.

■ Some states offer significant state tax savings for using your in-state plan.

■ Investments in a 529 Plan are managed by a fund manager You can't do your own stock picking.

■ The money in a 529 Plan is considered the asset of the contributor, which if it is not the beneficiary will have less negative impact on financial aid.

■ The money can only be used for college or graduate school expenses.

■ 529 Plans are not very flexible. There are restrictions on how often you can switch investment tracks and plans.

■ All 529 Plans are relatively new and have not established a long track record.

Prepaid Tuition Plans

■ These are relatively low-risk plans since you are guaranteed to have your tuition paid as long as you meet the schedule of payments.

■ Prepaid tuition plans are considered an asset of the parent (same as 529 Savings Plans) by the Federal methodology which means it will have a small impact on the student's financial aid.

■ Prepaid plans are not offered by all states. Your state college may not have a prepaid plan.

■ The plan locks you into a specific college system. If you are saving for a young child there is a chance that he or she may not want to go to your state college or that you may move to another state and not be able to transfer the fund.

■ Depending on your plan it may only cover tuition and not room and board, which is often a significant portion of college expenses.

463.

Take advantage of both Coverdell and 529 Savings Plans

There is no reason why you can't do both a Coverdell and 529 Savings Plan. This would give you some diversification of your savings since you have 100 percent control of your Coverdell investments. You can also use the Coverdell for primary and secondary expenses–especially if your child will be attending an expensive private high school.

Where can I find some calculators to help me plan my budget and savings?

The best calculators for figuring such things as how much you need to save for college and how much college will cost are found online. There are many good ones available. We like the calculators on SallieMae.com. They not only have the standard calculators but also some useful ones for creating a budget. Visit www.salliemae.com and look for the tools in the College Planning section.

Having a 529 Savings Plan will allow you to save more than the Coverdell since it has higher limits and you may be able to get more family members to participate by contributing. Depending on your state tax laws you may also enjoy some significant state tax deductions for using your state's own 529 Savings Plan.

Government Savings Bonds

464.

Cash in a bond tax-free

When we were kids, there was no birthday gift that was more disappointing than a savings bond. It was nice to see that the bond would be worth $100, but to have to wait five to seven years to redeem it seemed like an eternity. As a parent, however, you might want to consider buying bonds for your child's education since you may be able to exclude the interest earned from taxes if you use the proceeds to pay for qualified educational expenses.

Eligible bonds are series EE bonds issued on January 1990 and later, along with all Series I Bonds. To cash in the bonds tax-free you must have been at least 24 years old when you purchased them, and the bonds must be registered in your name or your spouse's name. Your child can be listed as a beneficiary but not as a co-owner. You must also meet specific income limits. For the 2018 tax year your modified gross adjusted income must be less than $79,550 if you are filing single and less than $119,300 if you file jointly. If you make more than this amount your tax benefits will be reduced. If you earn more than $94,550 as a single filer or $149,300 as a joint filer you cannot deduct any interest.

Unfortunately, savings bonds given to your child as a gift aren't eligible for tax-free treatment. Also, any bonds not purchased by you are similarly ineligible. However, if you meet the criteria all you need to do is file form 8815 to figure your education savings bond interest exclusion. For more information, take a look at http://www.savingsbonds.gov.

465.

Convert a savings bond to a 529 Savings Plan

Under the Education Bond Program you can cash in your bonds and use the proceeds to fund a 529 Savings Plan tax-free. The same limitations apply as in the above example of cashing in a bond to pay for educational expenses. You can learn more by visiting the Bureau of the Fiscal Service at https://www.fiscal.treasury.gov.

Gifting Money For College

466.

Gifting the old fashion way through UGMA/UTMA and Custodial Accounts

For a long time the Uniform Transfers/Gifts to Minors Acts were the main way parents and grandparents transferred money to a child. With money put into custodial accounts, children under the age of 18 can keep the first $1,050 in unearned income tax free and pay at their tax rate for the next $1,050. This also applies to children up to age 23 if they are full-time dependent students.

With the advent of 529 Savings Plans and the increased contribution limits to the Coverdell ESA, you now have an alternative to transfer money totally tax-free. The only limitation is that the money must be used to pay for educational expenses. If you want to help your child save for a down payment on a house or any non-education related uses, then UGMA/UTMA may still be the best option.

One additional potential advantage of transferring money with a 529 Plan is

that the money stays in your control. With a custodial account (and even Coverdell ESAs) the money becomes the property of the child at age 18 or 21, depending on your state's laws. Also, 529 Plans are considered the property of the contributor, which is usually the parent, while custodial accounts are the property of the student, which means that money will have a greater negative impact on the size of any financial aid package.

467.

For big money think Crummey Trust

When you hear the term "trust fund baby" it is usually referring to a Crummey Trust. This is the type of trust that you set up for a minor. Unlike with a custodial account, the person who sets up the trust fund can determine when the beneficiary is allowed to take control of the money. A Crummey Trust is usually established to hold a significant amount of money and is relatively expensive to establish. Plus, the trust is considered the asset of the beneficiary, which means it can hurt your chances of receiving financial aid. However, if you have a trust fund to begin with then there's a good chance you won't qualify for financial aid anyway.

Investing For College

If you choose to use a 529 Plan then most of your investment decisions are done. Once you pick which investment track you want to follow within your plan, the fund manager will take care of all the day-to-day decisions. Like a mutual fund you just keep adding money over time. However, if you plan to open a Coverdell or simply to invest on your own, you'll learn that investing for college is different than for other goals such as retirement. The biggest challenge is that you don't have as much flexibility over when you need the money. You can always defer retirement for five years but not so with a college education. Incorporate the following tips for your own investment strategies.

468.

Set annual goals

You need to know what your goal is before you start investing. Figure out how much college will cost when your child is ready to attend. Be sure to plan for both private and public college educations. Once you have a goal you can set targets for your investment strategy. Plus, as you get closer to your goal you can switch to an increasingly conservative strategy to make sure you don't risk what you worked so hard to build. To get a good estimate for what it will cost for your child to go to college in the future take a look at the college planning tools on the Sallie Mae website at http://www.salliemae.com. You might want to sit down before you view the final total.

469.

Start early to give your money time to grow

The hardest part of investing is often getting started. You need to fill out paper work to open accounts and select investment options, but the sooner you begin the better your chances are of reaching your goal. Time is on your side. Once you get your investments started you might want to consider making an automatic investment each month. Mutual funds, for example, let you set up automatic investment so that each month a certain amount of additional shares are purchased. But don't be tempted to set these mechanisms up and then forget about them. Pay attention and don't get complacent especially as the time for when you need the money approaches.

470.

Minimize your risk and maximize your return with dollar cost averaging

If you want to be conservative in your investment approach, consider the strategy of dollar cost averaging. This is based on the principle that the market in the long term always rises and trying to time the market is next to impossible. Therefore, it is best to buy a fixed amount of stock or mutual funds each month. Some months you are buying high since the market is up, but some months you are buying at a bargain when the market is down. Over time this will average out and you will have taken advantage of low prices while not investing your entire nest egg when the market was too high. Combined with an automatic investment option this can be a really low maintenance way to invest.

471.

Play it conservatively

You don't want to gamble with your child's future. While there is always risk in any kind of investment, make sure you are not being too aggressive when you are nearing the time you need the money. If you didn't learn your lesson from the dot-com implosion, don't speculate on so-called "sure bets" or "hot tips." Even relatively safe choices start to look too risky if you can't wait out a market downturn.

472.

Diversify to prevent putting all your eggs in one basket

Part of being conservative with your investments is diversifying your portfolio. You don't want to keep all of your money in one stock or even one sector. Spread your money around to make sure a collapse in one part of your portfolio won't sink your entire investment boat.

473.

Take a lesson from age-based 529 Savings Plans

Most 529 Plans offer a conservative age-based approach. When your child is young, the fund invests more aggressively in stocks and mutual funds. As your child gets older more money is shifted into fixed income investments like bonds. When your child is a few years from college most of the money is kept in safe money market funds. You don't want a disaster in the stock market to doom your child's chances of getting an education. As you near the time when you need the money, begin to move out of more risky investments.

474.

Don't neglect your IRAs

Compared to the Coverdell ESA or a good 529 Plan, using an Individual Retirement Account (IRA) is not the best way to save for college since you may have to pay taxes on what you withdraw. However, there are some benefits that make building your IRA a smart idea.

When it comes to determining financial aid, your retirement accounts are exempt from consideration. In other words, colleges can't touch these accounts when they try to determine how much money you can afford to pay for college. Plus, you can withdraw money from an IRA before you turn 59 ½ and avoid the 10 percent early withdrawal penalty as long as the money is used for college expenses. This applies to any IRA you own, whether it is a traditional IRA (including a SEP-IRA), a Roth IRA or a SIMPLE IRA. If you want to learn more about these different IRAs take a look at the IRS's Publication 590. Remember that you might have to pay income tax on part of the money that you withdraw, but at least you avoid the huge 10 percent penalty. Speak with your accountant to determine if this is a good strategy for you.

475.

Purchase zero coupon bonds strategically

These bonds are issued at a discount from their face value. After a specified maturity date the bond can be redeemed for the full face value. You will need to make sure that the maturity date is before the time when you need to use it for college. But these are relatively safe investments, and if you plan correctly you can have bonds mature at each year in which the tuition bills are due.

Saving Money Every Day

Cutting your family expenses means more money that you can save and invest. As the parent of a college-bound student you should be ruthless in your quest to cut family expenses to free up money to save. Here are some ways to do it:

476.

Don't ever think that it's too late to start saving

Given a choice, it is better to start saving for college when your child is 5 instead of 18. But don't throw up your hands in despair even if you have only a year or less to save. Because things like financial aid and scholarships are unpredictable, whatever you can save may be just enough to fill a critical gap. Also, every dollar you save could mean one less dollar you have to borrow. This will save you a lot of money in interest payments. When you think about it, each dollar you save is actually worth a lot more if it helps you borrow less. So no matter how soon you have to pay the first tuition bill, start saving money today.

One last benefit to saving early is that you also begin to train your family to live on less. Parents supporting a child in college can attest to the personal sacrifices they make. If you can learn to live on less now then these sacrifices won't seem as difficult.

How much do I have to save each month to be able to reach my goal?

The answer depends on how much your goal is. You want to sock away as much as possible. If you look at this chart you can see how much you will have if you save $50, $100, $250 and $500 per month. This table assumes a 5 percent growth rate on all of your money saved. As you can see, the amount you can save even with a limited budget and in a short amount of time can add up.

Number of years saved	Amount saved per month	Grand total
1	50	616
1	100	1,233
1	250	3,082
1	500	6,165
2	50	1,264
2	100	2,529
2	250	6,322
2	500	12,645
3	50	1,945
3	100	3,891
3	250	9,728
3	500	19,457
4	50	2,661
4	100	5,323
4	250	13,308
4	500	26,617
5	50	3,414
5	100	6,828
5	250	17,072
5	500	34,144
7	50	5,037
7	100	10,074
7	250	25,186
7	500	50,373
10	50	7,796
10	100	15,592
10	250	38,982
10	500	77,964

477.

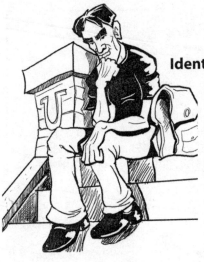

Identify and eliminate the non-essential luxuries

For many families the key to saving money is to cut unnecessary expenses. Here is a great exercise. Record for an entire month how much you spend. Write down every dollar you spend from food, to clothes, to going to the movies. At the end of the month add up what's on your list. Where is your money going? What expenses are non-essential or luxuries? Do you really need that $4 cappuccino when you could make it at home instead? Does your family need to eat out that often? It may seem trivial but we bet you can find more than spare change to save when you carefully examine how your family spends its money.

One family we know noticed that they were spending nearly $300 a month on restaurant and fast food. They switched to eating at home and doing barbecues when they wanted something special and were able to add more than $3,000 a year to their college savings.

478.

Put off the big purchases, if you can

Instead of buying a new car, push the old one a few more years. Sure a new kitchen would be nice but so would Johnny graduating without your having to take out a second mortgage. Remember too that big purchases also have long-term consequences. The new car will saddle you with higher insurance payments. Remodeling the bathroom may force you to take out a home equity loan. As long as the purchases are not essential (do spend the money to fix a leaky roof), consider putting them off until after your child graduates from college.

479.

Postpone college for a year to help you save

While we have been focused on ways to save for college, one often overlooked option is to have your child wait and work for a year. You can usually defer for a year before entering college. Doing so can also help you decide if college is the right choice. We know of several students who were not too enthusiastic about college until they took a year off and went to work. What they found in the work world was that without a college degree their future was severely limited. Taking a year off not only allowed them to save some money but it also got them excited about going to school.

If you are planning on taking a year off, we strongly recommend that you still apply to college during your senior year and then after you are accepted defer admission by a year. What this means is that you are already accepted by the college but simply postponing the start date. Your will need to talk to the admission office to make sure this is possible. Knowing that you have a guaranteed spot in college will save you a lot of stress.

Tax Breaks For Students

Get Your Tax Dollars Back

It is said that nothing is certain in life except death and taxes. If you are going to college or are the parent of a college-bound student, then you can add one more certainty to life and that is: tuition bills. Fortunately, Uncle Sam acknowledges this reality and offers several valuable tax credits and deductions. These tax breaks literally put money back in your pocket to help you pay those inevitable tuition bills.

The challenge with tax breaks is two-fold. First, you need to decipher the tax codes to determine if you actually qualify for a tax break. Most have income limits and other requirements that restrict their use. Second, if you qualify to take advantage of multiple tax breaks you need to figure out which combination will give you the most benefit. To complicate matters (and you shouldn't expect anything less from the IRS), some of these tax breaks are mutually exclusive, which means you'll have to choose one over the other.

Before you take advantage of any tax break, do a little long-term planning and create several scenarios to see how each choice affects your bottom line. As you will see there are some situations where electing to take a tax break may impact another area of your personal finances.

The information in this chapter is not meant to be authoritative tax advice or a guide to doing your taxes. Before you take advantage of a tax break, check with your accountant to make sure that you meet all qualifications and that the tax rules have not changed.

Timing Is Everything

The premise for all tax breaks is to refund you money that you have paid out of your pocket for college expenses. To claim a tax credit or deduction you therefore must have spent your own money on your or your child's education. That money can't come from a source that is already tax-free such as Coverdell ESA, scholarships, veteran educational assistance, Pell grants or 529 Savings

Plans. This is because any money that already receives favorable tax treatment cannot be claimed for an additional tax credit. Doing so is known as "double dipping," which is a big "no-no" to the IRS.

Since this is an important concept let's look at an example. Imagine that you have set up a 529 Savings Plan that has a balance of $15,000. During your child's first year of college you spent the entire contribution portion (this is the money you put in) of the 529 Plan so what's left represents the earnings portion. The earning portion is totally tax-free as long as you use it for educational expenses. It just so happens that tuition for this year is $15,000. If you use your entire 529 Savings Plan money to pay for tuition, you cannot claim any tax credits on what you have paid for tuition since you used money that already had a tax benefit. Remember the earnings portion of your 529 Plan is tax deferred. However, if you withdraw only $11,000 from the 529 Plan and pay the remaining $4,000 with money from your own pocket you could claim a tax credit on $4,000. If you use the American Opportunity tax credit (formerly the Hope tax credit) assuming that you meet the income limits, you receive the maximum amount of $2,500. Plus, you still have $4,000 left in your 529 Savings Plan for next year's tuition bill.

The bottom line is you need to plan in advance how you are going to take advantage of your tax breaks before you start paying for college. With a little planning you can dramatically affect the value of these tax breaks, leading to more money in your pocket to pay for college.

Remember too that tax laws as well as their interpretations change each year. Please check the requirements of these tax breaks by downloading the latest version of IRS publication 970 at http://www.irs.gov. With this caution in mind, let's take a look at some of the tax breaks that you may be able to use.

480.

Give yourself up to $2,500 with the American Opportunity tax credit

This tax credit reduces your taxes dollar for dollar and is like putting money directly into your pocket. You may receive up to $2,500 in tax

> **What's the difference between a tax credit and a tax deduction?**
>
> Tax credits reduce the amount of tax you owe dollar for dollar. Therefore, a tax credit of $1,000 means you will pay $1,000 less in taxes. A tax deduction reduces the amount of money on which your tax is calculated. A tax deduction of $1,000 may save you $200 in actual taxes depending on your tax bracket.

credits per student. The American Opportunity credit may be claimed in all four years of college.

To figure out how much of a American Opportunity tax credit that you can claim per student, look at the total amount of money that you paid out of your own pocket for tuition. The American Opportunity credit can only be used for tuition, not room and board and other expenses. So if you are using 529 or Coverdell money you'll want to use it to pay for room and board and use some of your own to pay for tuition. Once you know how much you've paid out of pocket for tuition, you can claim 100 percent of the first $2,000 and 25 percent of the next $2,000 that you paid. In other words to claim the full $2,500 per student you must have paid at least $4,000 in qualified education expenses for that student.

To claim the American Opportunity tax credit you must also meet the income requirements. For a single taxpayer you can get the full credit if your modified gross adjusted income does not exceed $80,000. If it does but is below $90,000 you can claim a partial credit. For married couples filing jointly you can get the full credit if your income does not exceed $160,000. If you earn more but are still below $180,000 you can claim a partial credit.

To claim a American Opportunity tax credit, file your taxes using Form 1040 or 1040A and attach Form 8863 Education Credits. There are a few other stipulations attached to the American Opportunity credit, which are that the student must be enrolled at least half-time, enrolled in a program that leads to a degree, certificate or other recognized educational credential and must be free of any felony conviction for possessing or distributing a controlled substance.

481.

If you're over the income limit you may get a partial credit
Like all tax credits, the American Opportunity has an income require-
ment. If you are over the initial limit, which is $80,000 for single filers
and $160,000 for joint filers, but still below the maximum limit, which
is $90,000 for single filers and $180,000 for joint filers, you can claim
a partial credit.

To figure out how much you can claim, take the amount that you are
over the limit and divide it by the phase-out range. This tells you by
what percentage you are over the initial limit. You can then take the
remaining percentage (the percentage by which you are still under the
maximum limit) and multiply it again by the American Opportunity
credit of $2,500 to figure out how much you can claim.

For example, if you are a single filer and you earn $83,000, you are
$3,000 over the initial limit of $80,000. You divide that $3,000 by the
phase-out range, which is $10,000. The phase-out range is simply the
difference between the maximum limit of $90,000 and the initial limit
of $80,000. This gives you 0.3, which means you are 30 percent over
the initial limit. You can therefore still claim up to 70 percent of the
credit or up to $1,750 ($2,500 maximum credit x 0.7 = $1,750.) The
process is the same for joint filers only now the phase-out range is
$20,000 since you take the difference between $180,000 and $160,000.

482.

Get up to $2,000 with the Lifetime Learning credit
The Lifetime Learning credit is similar to the American Opportunity
credit and reduces the tax you owe dollar for dollar. However, you
cannot claim both an American Opportunity and a Lifetime Learning credit on the same student in the same year. It is usually to your
advantage to claim the American Opportunity tax credit.

If you are an adult student who has already completed four years of
undergraduate work or are taking continuing education courses or if
you are a graduate school student, then you have no choice but to
take the Lifetime Learning credit.

The maximum amount of the Lifetime Learning credit is $2,000 per tax return, which is figured out by taking 20 percent of what you pay for tuition (not room and board or other expenses) up to $10,000. This means that to claim the full $2,000 credit, you must spend $10,000 or more out of your own pocket on tuition. Remember, money that is already receiving a tax benefit like the earnings portions of Coverdell and 529 Plans or tax-free scholarships don't count in figuring out how much you spent. The IRS doesn't allow double-dipping.

There are income limits for the Lifetime Learning credit. For a single taxpayer you can get the full credit if your modified gross adjusted income does not exceed $56,000. If it does but is below $66,000 you can claim a partial credit. For married couples filing jointly you can get the full credit if your income does not exceed $112,000. If you earn more but are still below $132,000 you can claim a partial credit.

Besides the income limit, you also must pay the tuition and related fees for an eligible student, which can include yourself, your spouse or a dependent for whom you claim an exemption on your tax return. The student does not, however, have to study toward a degree. Eligible courses can be part of a postsecondary degree program or taken by the student to acquire or improve job skills. Eligible educational institutions include any college, university, vocational school or other postsecondary educational institution eligible to participate in a student aid program administered by the Department of Education. This includes virtually all accredited, private or public, non-profit, and proprietary (privately owned, profit-making) postsecondary institutions.

Also, the felony drug conviction rule that might prevent you from getting an American Opportunity credit does not apply for the Lifetime Learning credit.

483.

Choose your tax credit wisely since you can only claim one per student per year

You can claim only one tax credit per student per year, which means you need to decide whether to claim the American Opportunity or

Lifetime Learning credit if you qualify for both. Generally it's better to claim the American Opportunity tax credit if you're eligible:

Lifetime Learning credit

- Up to $2,000 credit per return if you spent $10,000 or more of your own money on qualified tuition expenses. The amount that you can claim is less if you spent less. To figure the credit, take 20 percent of what you spent on qualified expenses up to the maximum of $10,000.

- You can claim a Lifetime Learning credit for all years of postsecondary education (including adult education) and for courses to acquire or improve job skills.

- You do not need to be pursuing a degree or other recognized educational credential.

- The felony drug conviction rule does not apply for the Lifetime Learning credit.

American Opportunity credit

- Up to $2,500 credit per eligible student. To get the maximum amount you must have spent at least $4,000 on qualified tuition expenses.

- If you qualify for both the American Opportunity and Lifetime Learning credits you probably want to take the American Opportunity since you'll receive a larger credit.

- You must be pursuing an undergraduate degree or other recognized educational credential.

- You must be enrolled at least half-time for at least one academic period.

- You cannot have any felony drug convictions.

484.

Be sure to get your tax credits in the right order

Since you can claim only one of the credits for each student per year, make sure you take advantage of them in the right order. If you qualify for both then you probably want to use the American Opportunity credit. The American Opportunity credit lets you qualify for the full amount while using less of your own money. This means you can spend more of your Coverdell or 529 Savings Plan money. In some cases this is a good idea since both affect your chances of receiving financial aid. If you have a large college savings this could adversely affect if or how much aid your child receives. By depleting this account in the first few years of college, you may increase your chances of getting financial aid in your child's last years in college.

485.

Don't carelessly miss getting your credit

If you've been diligently contributing to a 529 Savings Plan or Coverdell Education Savings Account, you may find that you have enough money to pay for all of your child's tuition in the first year. However, if you do this you may not be able to claim an American Opportunity tax credit. Since the earning portions of both 529 and Coverdell money are tax-free you can't claim an American Opportunity tax credit for using them. To get around this, you need to pay for some of the tuition expenses with money that does not come from your 529 or Coverdell accounts or that comes from the contribution part of your 529 or Coverdell since this is money that you've already paid taxes on. If you do this (and pay the rest using your tax-free money) you will be able to claim the tax credit.

486.

Lower your income to claim a tax credit

If you are over the income limits that trigger a phase-out for any tax break, you may be able to change your modified gross adjusted income just enough to qualify for the full credit or a larger partial credit. The key is to boost your "above the line" contributions. If you look at your 1040 tax return you'll notice that your adjusted gross income is on line 37. Anything that appears on lines 23 through 36 are known as "above the line" deductions which will reduce your AGI. For most people the one item they have the most control over is contributions to IRAs including SEP and SIMPLE IRAs. Also, contributions to 401k, 403b or 457 retirement plans reduce your income reported on your W2 and have the same effect of reducing your AGI. By increasing your contributions to these accounts you will lower your adjusted gross income. This might be enough to give you a bigger slice of the tax break pie. Plus, money in your retirement accounts is sheltered from the financial aid calculations, which can increase your chances of getting more financial aid from the college.

487.

Don't forget you can deduct your student loan interest

Tax deductions are not as good as tax credits but they do reduce your taxable income, which means you will still pay less taxes. One of the most common education deductions is for student loan interest. All student loan interest that you pay is tax deductible up to $2,500 per year. The loan must have been used for qualified higher-education expenses, including tuition, fees, room and board, supplies and other related expenses. Also the maximum allowable deduction is gradually reduced for single taxpayers whose modified gross adjusted income exceeds $65,000 but is below $80,000 and for married taxpayers filing jointly whose MAGI exceeds $135,000 but is below $165,000.

You can usually count as interest the loan-origination fees (other than fees for services), capitalized interest, interest on revolving lines of credit and interest on refinanced student loans, which include both consolidated loans and collapsed loans. You can also count any voluntary interest payments that you make. To claim the deduction you should receive Form 1098-E from your lender or loan servicer.

488.

Deduct work-related education

Work-related education may provide you with a tax deduction if it amounts to more than two percent of your adjusted gross income. The education must also meet one of these two tests: it is required by your employer or the law to keep your current job, or it maintains or improves skills necessary in your current work.

You must also be working and itemize your deductions on Schedule A if you are an employee. Self-employed workers must file Schedule C, Schedule C-EZ or Schedule F. The great benefit of this deduction is that you may utilize it even if the education could lead to a degree.

489.

Educational benefits from your employer may be tax-free

If you have a generous employer you might be able to receive up to $5,250 of tax-free employer provided educational assistance benefits each year. This means that you may not have to pay tax on amounts your employer pays for your education including payments for tuition, fees and similar expenses, books, supplies and equipment. This can be used for both undergraduate and graduate-level courses. Plus, the payments do not have to be for work-related courses.

How do I calculate my modified adjusted gross income (MAGI) to see if I can deduct what I paid for tuition and fees?

For most taxpayers, your modified adjusted gross income is simply your adjusted gross income (AGI) on your tax return. If you file Form 1040, your MAGI is the AGI on line 37 without taking into account any amount on lines 34 or 35 (tuition and fees deduction or domestic production activities deduction.) You must add back to your income any foreign earned income exclusion, foreign housing exclusion, foreign housing deduction and the exclusion of income from American Samoa or Puerto Rico.

However, you cannot use any of the tax-free education expenses paid for by your employer as the basis for any other deduction or credit, including the American Opportunity and Lifetime Learning credits.

490.

Cash in your government bonds tax-free

If you cashed in a government savings bond to pay for qualified educational expenses you may be able to exclude the interest earned from your federal incomes taxes. The key is that you must have purchased a series EE bond issued after 1989 or the series I bond. The bond must be issued either in your name or in the name of both you and your spouse. You must have been at least 24 years old at the time when you purchased the bond, and it cannot have been a gift to or be in the name of your child.

If you meet these requirements and your modified adjusted gross income is less than $79,550 if filing a single return or $119,300 if filing a joint return you can deduct the interest used to pay for tuition. If your modified gross income is higher than these amounts but below $94,550 for single filers and $149,300 for joint filers then you will still be able to exclude a portion of the interest. You will need to file Form 8815 to figure out your education savings bond interest exclusion.

491.

Money-saving tax benefits of scholarships and fellowships

If you received an academic scholarship or fellowship that is used for qualified tuition, fees and books then it is generally not taxable. For a scholarship or fellowship to be non-taxable you must meet the following conditions:

- You are a candidate for a degree at an educational institution,
- The amounts you receive as a scholarship or fellowship must be used for tuition and fees required for enrollment or attendance at the educational institution, or for books, supplies and equipment required for courses of instruction and
- The amounts received are not a payment for your services.

You cannot exclude from your taxable income any scholarships or grants that are used to pay for room and board.

492.

Get more tax help

Tax questions are never easy and it is essential that you talk to a professional accountant. In addition, tax laws are constantly changing. To get the latest (and free) information, surf over to the IRS website at http:// www.irs.gov or schedule phone or personal appointment. You can call with questions to 800-829-1040, or try the IRS's Everyday Tax Solutions service by calling your local IRS office to set up an in-person appointment. If you have access to TTY/TDD equipment, call 800-829-4059.

How do I calculate my modified adjusted gross income (MAGI) to see if I can deduct my student loan interest payments?

For most taxpayers, your modified adjusted gross income is the adjusted gross income (AGI) from your federal income tax return before subtracting any deduction for student loan interest. If you file Form 1040A, your MAGI is the AGI on line 21 without taking into account any amount on line 18 (student loan interest deduction.) If you file Form 1040, your MAGI is the AGI on line 37 without taking into account any amount on line 33 (student loan interest deduction) or line 35 (Domestic production activities or tuition and fees deduction.) You must add back to your income any foreign earned income exclusion, foreign housing exclusion, foreign housing deduction and the exclusion of income from American Samoa or Puerto Rico.

Glossary

IRS Form 970: This is the form from the IRS that outlines tax benefits for education including scholarships, fellowships, grants and tuition reductions; the American Opportunity tax credit; the Lifetime Learning tax credit; student loan interest deduction; student loan cancellations and repayment assistance; tuition and fees deduction; Coverdell Education Savings Accounts; the Qualified Tuition Program (QTP); the Education Savings Bond Program; employer-provided educational assistance and business deductions for work-related education. The form is available at http://www.irs.gov/publications/p970.

Modified adjusted gross income (MAGI): For most, your MAGI is the adjusted gross income (AGI) from your federal income tax return before subtracting any deduction for student loan interest.

Tax credit: Tax credits reduce the amount of tax you owe dollar for dollar. With a tax credit of $2,500, you will pay $2,500 less in taxes.

Tax deduction: Tax deductions reduce the amount of money on which your tax is calculated. If you are in the 28 percent tax bracket, a tax deduction of $1,000 will save you $280.

Maximize Financial Aid

Get Your Share Of Financial Aid

Federal Financial aid can seem like a big, scary mystery. We've actually met people who had nightmares about it. One involved a despotic financial aid officer sitting on top of an 800-foot high pile of cash. Below, a line of weary parents waited their turn. A lucky few received a small handful of dollars. But most got nothing and walked away with bowed heads. Fortunately, this was just a dream. Reality is far less dark and mysterious. You see financial aid officers are not your arch enemies but your allies in helping you pay for college.

The financial aid system has evolved over many decades and is based on a set of well-established rules. If you understand these rules you will not only feel more in control of the process but you will also insure that you have the best chance to get the most financial aid that you deserve.

The Philosophy of Financial Aid

Before we introduce you to the rules, you need to understand one important philosophical principle about financial aid. It is that a college education is not an entitlement. In other words, unlike a high school education, the government does not guarantee anyone the right to an affordable college education. The government does believe that it is in the best interest of society at large to make college as accessible as possible to the most number of people. So it provides aid but only after you have exhausted nearly all of your own resources. Financial aid is not designed to help you spend less money on college but rather to help you afford to go to a college that you might not have been able to pay for on your own. You also have to keep in mind that since a college education is not an entitlement there is no guarantee that even if you meet every qualification that the government or college will automatically come to your aid.

In practical terms this means that while you should apply for financial aid, you should not view it as a sure thing that will take care of the bills you can't afford. Think of yourself as a mountain climber who has a 90-foot rope. If you want to scale a 110-foot cliff then financial aid might give you that extra 20 feet of rope to do so. But if you want to climb a 150-foot cliff you will find that even with the extra 20 feet of rope from financial aid, you still need to bring more of your own rope. Of course, you can also decide to climb a lower cliff.

Okay, enough with the analogies. Let's see how financial aid works and how to get the most you deserve.

The FAFSA and CSS/PROFILE

The primary job of the college financial aid officer is to look at your family's finances and determine your "financial need." To do so they need to get a sense of your family finances. You will provide this information on a form called the *Free Application for Federal Student Aid* or FAFSA. Using your prior-prior year (PPY) tax returns, you will reveal all of the money that you have in savings, investments and hidden Swiss bank accounts. If you are applying to a private college you may also have to provide additional information through the college's own financial aid form or the College Board's *CSS/Financial Aid PROFILE* form. Like the FAFSA, it asks similar questions about your finances.

You can download a copy of these forms and even complete them online at http://www.fafsa.ed.gov for the FAFSA and http://www.collegeboard.com for the PROFILE.

With a detailed picture of your financial situation, each college financial aid officer will analyze the money you have and based on the cost of the college will figure out your degree of financial need. Once they know how much you need, they put together a financial aid package, which spells out how much and from where you are to get this money.

But first, let's begin by looking at how the colleges figure out that magical number of how much money your family can afford to pay for college.

Step 1: Learn How To Qualify For Financial Aid

The first step to getting financial aid is to understand how the system works. Once you know how the calculations determine if you qualify for financial aid you can look at ways to make sure you are getting the most aid you deserve.

493.

Understand how the Institutional and Federal methodologies determine how much you will pay

Public and private colleges have adopted different formulas and procedures for determining how much money your family can afford to pay for college. Public schools (and some privates, too) use what is known as the Federal methodology. This is the formula provided by the U.S. Department of Education. When you submit the Free Application for Federal Student Aid (FAFSA), the government uses the information you provide to calculate the amount of money that you can put toward college for one year. The Federal methodology looks at things like your income and assets but does not consider assets such as retirement accounts and equity that you have built up in your home.

Some private colleges want to know about your retirement accounts and home equity and will use the Institutional methodology. By completing the College Board's PROFILE form in addition to the FAFSA you will give the colleges some additional financial information. While the Institutional methodology is somewhat stricter than the Federal methodology and will usually result in less financial need, you really don't have a choice in the matter since you need to submit the financial aid applications the colleges require.

The goal of both the Federal and Institutional methodologies is to take the numbers you provide on the FAFSA and PROFILE forms, run a series of calculations and end up with a single number. This number is known as your Expected Family Contribution (EFC). This is the magic number. It represents the amount of money that your family is expected to contribute for one year of your education. This number can range from $0 to infinity.

About three to five days after you submit the FAFSA you will receive the Student Aid Report (SAR), which will tell you your Expected Family Contribution. You might want to be sitting down before you view your SAR. For the PROFILE you will not be told your Expected Family Contribution, but you can guess that it will be somewhat higher than the number on your Student Aid Report.

It's important to understand that the Expected Family Contribution is calculated by simply feeding the numbers you provide into a computer. Every family's situation is run through the same calculation. Two families with identical numbers on their FAFSA will have the same Expected Family Contributions. There are no special circumstances or explanations needed at this stage. It won't do you any good to send a letter along with your FAFSA describing how tough it is for your family to make ends meet. Save that letter for the next step when you deal directly with the financial aid officers at the colleges. At this point you are just providing accurate information on your finances based on your tax returns.

But the game is just beginning. Once your Expected Family Contribution has been determined, it is passed on to the colleges you have applied to or the college you attend and is used to determine if you have financial need. It is also at the college level where the exact composition of your financial aid package is determined. And, it is at this point that the computers are turned off and human beings take over.

494.

How your magic number–a.k.a. your Expected Family Contribution–is determined

At this point you are probably wondering how in the heck the government uses a snapshot of your family's finances to determine how much you can spend on college. Like everything from taxes to Social Security benefits, to calculate your Expected Family Contribution the government uses a formula. Here is the general formula, which can change from year to year, for computing your EFC.

Parents' adjusted income x (up to 47 percent) +
Parents' assets x (up to 5.65 percent) +

Student's income x (up to 50 percent) +
Student's assets x (20 percent) = Expected Family Contribution

There are some factors such as family size and number of children in college at the same time that the government uses to adjust the exact percentage that it will assess against your income and assets. Also, there are income and asset protection figures that prevent the government from touching everything that you have. While we could go into a lot of detail to show you the nitty gritty detail of the calculation, we feel it's better that you have a solid overview since that will help you understand how to get more financial aid.

If you want a really detailed calculation to forecast your Expected Family Contribution then we recommend you use an online EFC calculator. One good calculator is on the College Board website at http://bigfuture.collegeboard.org. You can play with it and try different numbers to simulate various changes in your finances. If you want to do it yourself on paper, you can download an EFC worksheet at https://ifap.ed.gov. Click on the heading "Worksheets, Schedules and Tables."

What is the timeline for applying for financial aid?

September-December
Focus on your college applications if you are still in high school.

After October 1
Complete and submit your financial aid applications.

After submitting FAFSA
Review your Student Aid Report, which will be sent to you after you submit your FAFSA.

April
You should receive both your college acceptance letters and financial aid packages. Review and compare your aid packages. Ask for a reassessment, if necessary.

May
This is the typical deadline for accepting all or part of your financial aid package.

But for now let's keep things simple and just consider the above formula. Right away you can see that parents' income, student's income and student's assets are the most heavily assessed. Since most students have low to no income, the heavy factors are really parents' income and student's assets. If you can lower either of these numbers, you may be able to significantly change your Expected Family Contribution.

Before we look at how to lower your Expected Family Contribution, we need to point out just a few more things about what counts as income and assets. When you pay your taxes you don't get taxed on everything that you make. You make deductions and shelter some of your money from the tax collector. The same is true when calculating your Expected Family Contribution. Let's take a quick look at what are legitimate debts that will reduce your income or assets in the eyes of financial aid.

495. Your family expense sheet does not count as debt for financial aid

Debt has always been a touchy subject. Colleges are very strict about what they consider debt that can reduce your income. They will not subsidize a family's expensive habits. If a family makes $8,000 a month in income but has expenses of $7,500 a month for such things as car payments, gardener bills, annual family trips to Europe, dinners at the finest restaurants, payments for the big screen TV, etc. then that's too bad. All of these discretionary expenses are not used to reduce your income. Be careful how you think about your income, and don't assume that your family expenses will be taken out when figuring out your income. The financial aid formula will apply the same income protection number (which is quite conservative) to all families. If most of your paycheck is spent in the same month you receive it, you are going to be surprised at how much the financial aid formula will expect you to pay. If, on the other hand, you are controlling expenses and saving your money, you'll find that the expectations are far more reasonable.

496. Credit card debt is not debt when it comes to the financial aid calculation

If you need one more reason not to carry credit card debt (besides the high interest rate) consider the fact that any credit card balances and interest paid will not lower your income for the purposes of financial aid. In reality these debts certainly take money from your pockets. Many families with high consumer debt are surprised at how much money colleges think they can afford. Remember that these debts are considered discretionary and often reflect a family's living style rather than a necessity.

497. Car payments will not lower your income

Car payments will not lower your income for financial aid. Therefore, the lower your payments the better. If you have a choice, pick a less-expensive car and avoid financing.

498. Mortgage payments will not lower your income

Under both the Federal and Institutional methodologies your home mortgage or home equity loan payments will not reduce your income. The same is true for a passbook loan. However, unlike credit card interest payments you can deduct your mortgage or home equity loan payments from your taxes.

499. Your savings and checking accounts are assets

Under both the Federal and Institutional methodologies anything in your savings or checking accounts are counted as assets that you can use to pay for college. If you look at the calculations you'll notice that compared to income these assets are assessed at a much lower rate. There is no legal way to hide these assets.

500. Your stock and bond portfolios are assets

Under both the Federal and Institutional methodologies any stocks or bonds that you hold, which are not in retirement accounts, are fair game for the colleges to assess as available to pay for college. You should not radically alter your investment strategy or holdings just to get a few extra bucks from financial aid. It is just not worth the trouble, and you'll probably lose more than you'll gain.

501. Your house may or may not be an asset

Under the Federal methodology your home is not considered an asset. However, under the Institutional methodology a portion of your home's value may be considered an asset. This presents an interesting option. If you move money from your savings

Where do I get the FAFSA?

You can get your Free Application for Federal Student Aid by visiting http://www.fafsa.ed.gov or by calling 800-4-FED-AID. Most counseling offices and financial aid offices also have FAFSA forms available.

account, for example, into your home by adding a new roof you are effectively sheltering your assets from at least the Federal methodology and possibly also the Institutional methodology for calculating your Expected Family Contribution. But, and this is a big downside, you are spending money that you might need to pay for college. Remember there is no guarantee that the college will be able to fund your entire financial need. Also, as you will see, financial aid may come in the form of a loan, which would cost you more than if you had just used your savings.

However, consider the case where you have a leaky roof that needs to be replaced. It's your child's junior year in college. If you replace your roof now, as opposed to a year from now, you will reduce your savings account (i.e. your assets) and therefore make yourself more eligible for a higher financial aid package for your child's senior year. If you wait a year then it will be too late since your child will already be in the last year of college. (Remember, financial aid is always based on the previous tax year.) All of this assumes that you are already receiving aid and that you don't need the roof money to pay for living necessities. If you desperately need the money for something else, then it would be better to just live with the bucket in the living room until after your child graduates.

502. Retirement accounts cannot be touched

Under most circumstances money in retirement accounts will not be counted as an asset and therefore cannot be touched by the colleges. Stocks, bond and mutual funds held in normal accounts, even if you intend to use them for retirement, will be counted as an asset. To shelter your retirement money, you need to have it in an IRA or 401k type account.

503.

A quick estimate of your Expected Family Contribution

Income is the biggest determinant of Expected Family Contribution. The following chart shows average Expected Family Contribution levels from Troy Onink/Stratagee.

Family income	Average EFC 1 dependent	2 dependents
$50,000	$4,004	$3,081
$75,000	$10,455	$8,719
$100,000	$18,731	$17,168
$125,000	$25,677	$24,165
$150,000	$33,967	$31,933
$175,000	$41,802	$39,819
$200,000	$49,598	$47,615

Obviously, these are just average numbers based on a sample student population. Within each income level is a range of specific Expected Family Contribution amounts. You can get a more accurate estimate of your specific EFC by using an online EFC calculator and plugging in your actual family finances.

504.

Compute your EFC online–fast and easy

If you want to run a simulation to see what your Expected Family Contribution is, you can do so easily online. One good EFC calculator that we like is at the College Board website. Fill in what you know about your family's finances and it will compute your EFC according to both the Federal and Institutional methods. Find the calculator at https://bigfuture.collegeboard.org/pay-for-college/paying-your-share/expected-family-contribution-calculator.

505.

How to determine your financial need

Once you know your Expected Family Contribution, it's easy to determine your financial need. All you do is take the total cost of attending a specific college including tuition, room and board, books and travel expenses and subtract it from your Expected Family Contribution. The difference is your financial need. It's important to remember that individual schools, not you, determine the total cost of attendance.

Let's look at an example and assume that your college costs $25,000 per year for tuition and room and board. Add the average expenses for books, travel and miscellaneous expenses and the total cost of attendance may be $30,000 per year. You have submitted both the FAFSA and PROFILE forms. This means that the college has received your Expected Family Contribution as determined by the Federal and Institutional methodology. For argument's sake let's assume that under the Federal methodology your Expected Family Contribution is $15,000 and under the Institutional methodology it is $16,000. (Remember the Institutional methodology is usually stricter.) If the school only uses the Federal methodology it will take the $30,000 for the total cost of attendance and subtract the $15,000 that your family is expected to contribute. That leaves your family with a financial need of $15,000. If the school is a private college that uses the Institutional methodology, your financial need is $14,000.

It is this amount, your financial need, which the school must now figure out a way for your family to afford. They can give you money in the form of grants, student loans and work-study. Or, it is possible that the school won't be able to find all of the money, leaving you with "unmet need." The exact composition of your financial aid package will depend on a variety of factors and will vary by college. This is one benefit of applying to a number of colleges so that you can compare different financial aid packages.

Step 2: Lower Your Expected Family Contribution

Now that you understand how the financial aid formula works and what counts and doesn't count, you can use this information to try to lower your Expected Family Contribution. It's very important to remember that the following are generalized strategies that may not be appropriate for your individual situation. These are not solid rules since what might be good for one family may be terrible for another. Before taking any action, you should speak with your accountant to make sure that the strategy will work for your family's individual financial situation.

506.

Keep your child poor

If you look at the calculation for Expected Family Contribution you can see that if you put money into a child's name it will be assessed by 20 percent. But if you keep the money in your name it will only be assessed by up to 5.65 percent. That means for every $100 in the student's name you will be expected to spend $20 to pay for college. However, for every $100 in your name, you will be expected to pay only $5.65 to pay for college. That's a big difference. Any money that is in your child's bank account is considered your child's asset. If a relative would like to give a gift of cash or stock to your child you might want to ask if they are willing to either give it to you or wait until your child graduates from college. Or your generous relative could make the gift directly to your child's 529 Savings Plan.

Here is a chart of common savings accounts and how they are viewed by financial aid formulas:

- 529 Savings Plans (including pre-paid tuition plans) are an asset of the contributor, which is usually the parent.
- Coverdell Education Savings Accounts are an asset of the parents under the Federal and Institutional methodology.
- Custodial accounts are an asset of the student.
- Trust funds are an asset of the student.
- Savings bonds in the name of the student are an asset of the student.

Putting money in your child's name is generally a bad idea when it comes to financial aid. Of course, there may be some good tax reasons for putting money in your child's name especially if you know that

Is it worth it to spend my time filling out an application for financial aid?

The short answer is: "ABSOLUTELY!" While it does take some time to fill out a financial aid application, the benefits are well worth the effort. Not only do you try to claim your share of the more than $252 billion in aid that is awarded each year, but you also protect yourself against any future changes to your family's finances. By turning in a financial aid application, you give the college a snapshot of your finances. Should something change in the future this snapshot will be invaluable in helping the college understand how your family is impacted by the change, making it easier for them to respond with additional financial aid.

you won't qualify for financial aid. You need to balance the desire to save on taxes with the effect that putting money into a child's name will have on financial aid. It's important to speak with your accountant about your family's individual situation.

507.

Spend UGMA funds three years before your child graduates

Let's say that you have put some money into a custodial account for your child. Why not spend this money while your child is still in high school instead of leaving it to be counted against your financial need? Now if you go crazy and just spend it on things you normally would not have bought, then this won't help. However, let's say that when your child turns 16 and gets his or her license you plan to buy a used car for travel between school and work. Instead of using your own money, let the child use his or her custodial account. As long as you don't spend more than you normally would and buy a BMW instead of a Corolla, then you'll put your child in a better position to receive more financial aid. With the Coverdell, you can't buy a car but you can spend it on any legitimate high school educational expense such as books, uniforms and even a computer.

If you plan to do this, make sure you spend whatever you plan to before January 1 of your student's sophomore year. Remember financial aid is two years behind and you will submit account information based on the prior prior year's tax returns, which for the typical student who enters college in the fall will cover January 1 of the sophomore year through December 31 of the junior year.

508.

Consider deferring bonuses and raises

Imagine this scenario. It's November 2018 and your child is graduating from high school and starting college in the fall of 2020. Your boss tells you that you will get a bonus or significant raise. If you take the bonus now, then that money will be used when determining your child's financial aid package for the 2020-21 school year. Remember

---

In the case of a divorce whose income needs to be reported?

In most divorce situations the financial aid information must come from the parent with whom the student lives the most during the year. Some colleges also require that the non-custodial natural parent complete a separate aid application and these colleges will use their financial information in the aid calculation.

If the parent with whom the student lives remarries, then information must also be included from the stepparent. Regardless of whether or not the stepparent has any intention of supporting the child, his or her financial information will be used when determining financial aid.

The college will consider any special circumstances including if you are not able to locate the non-custodial natural parent. It's important that you communicate any special situations to the financial aid office.

financial aid is always based on the prior prior tax year. If you delay taking your bonus for two months until January 2019, then that money will not be used in your student's financial aid calculations. It will be counted when he or she applies for financial aid for the second year of college. But since you will have spent some (maybe even a significant amount) to pay for the first year you will have fewer assets that will be counted during the second year of college. This also buys you some time to save since you know that the bonus or increase in salary will reduce your financial aid in the following year.

Before you do this, be sure that you are going to get financial aid in the first place. Also consider other factors. Will your boss still be in the mood to give you a bonus next year? Sometimes it's better to just take the money.

This tactic would be much more effective if your child were entering the senior year in college in the fall of 2020. Deferring your raise or bonus in this situation would mean that it would not be counted at all since your son or daughter would be graduating from college.

509.

Consider alternative forms of bonuses

If you have the flexibility, it may make sense to take your bonus or even a pay raise in some other form than cash. Of course, if you need the money then take the cash, but if you are in a situation where there is an equally useful alternative then you might want to take it.

For example, instead of taking a raise you might swap one day a week of working from home which might save you money in other ways such as less childcare costs. Or you might convert your bonus from a cash payment to having your company pay for training or classes that you were planning to pay yourself. A bonus or raise that does not show up as income will not be subjected to financial aid consideration. However, carefully weigh the costs of forgoing a cash bonus or raise. If you can use the money to pay down credit card debt, for example, you are probably much better off doing that.

510.

Time your stock sales

When you sell a stock can have an impact on your financial aid. Let's say you have a stock that has appreciated by $10,000. If you sell the stock after January 1 of your child's sophomore year in high school, the earnings are considered income for your child's first year of college and will be assessed at up to 47 percent. That means that from the $10,000 gain as much as $4,700 can be counted by the financial aid formula as going to pay for college. But let's say that instead you sell the stock before January 1 of your child's sophomore year. The proceeds will not be counted as income but instead show up as an asset. As a parental asset this money can only be assessed at up to 5.65 percent, which means only $565 is considered as available to pay for college.

511.

Build your 401K or IRA accounts

Under both the Federal and Institutional methodologies your retirement accounts are not considered assets that can be used to pay for college. Plus, under current tax laws you can withdraw money from these accounts and use them to pay for college without paying a penalty. So don't neglect your retirement as you save for college.

512.

Declaring your independence

In college, you no longer have a curfew or parents telling you what to do, so why shouldn't you declare yourself independent? Many students mistakenly believe that if they declare their independence from their parents they will get more financial aid. Unfortunately, declaring independence for the purposes of financial aid is based on very strict guidelines. In most cases, you are considered dependent on your parents for support and their income and assets will be considered when determining your financial need. Under certain circumstances, you can be evaluated independently of your parents, and only you and your spouse's (if you have one) income and assets will be taken into account. You're considered independent if one of the following is true:

- You are 24 years or older by December 31 of the current year.
- You're married.
- You're enrolled in a graduate or professional degree program.
- You have legal dependents other than a spouse.
- You're an orphan or ward of the court.
- You're currently serving on active duty in the U.S. Armed Forces.
- You're a veteran of the U.S. Armed Forces.

Your parents may not support you at all, but according to the above guidelines you are still considered a dependent. If this is the case it is vitally important that you include a detailed letter explaining the situation to the college financial aid office.

Step 3: Complete The Financial Aid Application

Since we know you are going to be applying for financial aid, here are a few tips to make sure to fill out the applications correctly and present an accurate picture of your finances to the colleges

513.

Get into the right mindset

When you're sitting in front of the computer, you may have a feeling of dread at the thought of filling out the FAFSA. Tell yourself that it usually takes about 30 to 60 minutes to complete the form. When you think about it, that's a small investment of time for the possible reward!

514.

Colleges run out of money so turn in applications early
The deadlines for turning in your financial aid applications vary by college. You want to turn in your FAFSA as soon as possible after October 1, which if you are applying for aid for the first time is of your senior year in high school. The reason is that colleges have a limited amount of financial aid.

Most colleges use what is known as a "priority" deadline. While the deadline varies by school it is usually sometime in January or February. This date is when the school expects to run out of money. If you get your application turned in by this deadline you should be fine. However, if you application arrives late, or if it was somehow incomplete and you needed to provide more information that pushed you past this deadline, then even if you deserve aid you may not get it simply because the college ran out of money.

515.

Think about financial aid early–before your child is even in high school
Remember that all of the numbers used in financial calculations come from the prior prior tax year. If your child is starting college in September 2020, then your tax return from 2018 will be the basis for that first year. Therefore, if you wait until January 2019 to think about financial aid, it will be too late to do anything that will affect the outcome of your child's first year.

516.

Regardless of your income, don't assume that you won't get any financial aid
The biggest mistake that most families make when it comes to financial aid is they assume they won't qualify and therefore don't make the

> ### When should I apply for financial aid?
>
> Apply for financial aid as soon as possible after October 1 of your senior year if you're in high school. Don't wait until after you are accepted by a college to apply. If you do the college may have already allocated all of its money. When it comes to financial aid the early bird does get the worm.

effort to apply. You'll never know what you truly deserve unless you apply. You might find that even if you don't get a grant, you are awarded a cushy campus job, special college scholarships or low-interest student loan. You might find that one of these sources of money is just what you need to make paying for college possible.

Here's a chart from a recent U.S. Department of Education study. It is not surprising that as income rises the percentage of students who received financial aid decreases. But even for families that earned over $100,000 per year, more than 78 percent of them still received financial aid.

Family income	Percent of students who received financial aid
Below $20,000	96.1 percent
$20,000-40,000	94.3 percent
$40,000-60,000	92.4 percent
$60,000-80,000	87.1 percent
$80,000-100,000	83.4 percent
Above $100,000	78.6 percent

Another study conducted by an independent education advocacy group found that among today's current college students more than 850,000 qualified to receive federal grants. However, none of these students received a single dime from Uncle Sam. The reason? Because they didn't apply!

The bottom line is that it's dangerous to second-guess the financial aid office. Applying is free and won't take that much time. The rewards can be well worth the effort.

517.

Use your financial aid application as an insurance policy

Nobody can predict the future. Today you may have a great job, but next year you may be out of a job. Or perhaps an elderly grandparent may need to live with your family. Or maybe you will decide to stop working and go back to school. The future is uncertain, which means if something should happen to your family's finances during the year you will want to be able to approach the financial aid office to ask for some help. Your best chance of getting help will depend on whether or not you have applied for financial aid. Without having a FAFSA on record the college has no idea how much of an impact your family has sustained. It makes it much easier for a financial aid officer to give you more money if you have already filled out the FAFSA regardless of whether or not you were given any aid. So think of applying for aid as added insurance against any unexpected changes in your family's future finances.

518.

You must apply for financial aid every year

Financial aid is determined on a year-by-year basis. That means that even if you didn't get financial aid this year you should apply next year since your finances will have changed, especially after paying for one year of tuition. Some families find that after the first or second year of college they have reduced their assets to the point where they qualify for financial aid. There is a Renewal FAFSA that you can use, which saves a lot of time when applying for aid the next year.

519.

Get help completing the FAFSA

If you need help completing the FAFSA, visit the U.S. Department of Education website at http://www.fafsa.ed.gov or call 800-4-FED-AID. The website will take you step by step through the entire process. You might also want to contact your high school counselor or even the financial aid office at your local college. High schools and colleges often hold workshops throughout the spring to help parents and students complete the FAFSA.

Step 4: Work With The Financial Aid Office

All of the information that is used to compute your financial need either through the Federal or Institutional Methodology will eventually be sent to the college financial aid office. There a professional known as the financial aid office will review your information and make the final decision about how much money you will receive. The financial aid officer is an important ally and it's crucial that you know how to work with this professional.

520.

There is a human being behind all financial aid decisions

Up until this point financial aid looks very analytical. It seems like you just plug in the numbers and out pops your Expected Family Contribution. But the story of financial aid does not end with your Expected Family Contribution. After your EFC is computed, the rest of the process becomes a very human process. Your EFC will be sent to every college you are applying to, and this is where the computations end and human beings take over.

At the colleges, financial aid officers use your EFC as a guide when putting together your aid package. The financial aid officer has the ability to raise or lower your EFC for a variety of reasons. Therefore, it is crucial that you are open about your family's true financial situation to the financial aid officer. Remember, too, that all financial aid is based on your prior prior year's taxes. A lot may have happened since then. If you want to share additional information, you can send a letter to the college financial aid office to explain any unusual circumstances that may affect your family's finances. Most colleges actually include a space on their financial aid forms for you to describe any relevant information. When you are thinking about writing this letter consider the following three points.

521. Don't hide the dirty laundry

Many parents when filling out financial forms feel compelled to hide embarrassing circumstances. After all you are revealing your financial strengths and weaknesses to a total stranger. However, if you have extraordinary circumstances such as large medical bills, unemployment, recent or ongoing divorce, siblings attending private elementary or high schools or any additional expenses that may not be reflected in your FAFSA or PROFILE, tell the financial aid officer. Don't be embarrassed. It could cost you big time.

522. Give the college a reason to give you more money

Financial aid officers are numbers people. However, they have wide latitude for interpreting numbers and can apply a variety of standards and make exceptions, which can help or hurt your case. To get the most support from these professionals, make your case with numbers. You can't just say that you don't have enough money. You need to show it. Document with numbers why your tax forms don't accurately reflect your true income or expenses.

523. Be prepared to show the evidence

It's not enough to say that your income has dropped significantly, you need to show it with documentation. Get all your paperwork in order so if the financial aid office requests documentation, you have it.

524. Don't ever try to trick the college

The human being in the financial aid process is also what keeps it safe from trickery. You could, for example, take all of the money in your savings account and plunk it down to buy

Should I do the FAFSA online?

Yes, we do recommend that you complete the FAFSA online at http://www.fafsa.ed.gov. The online form will help check calculations and alert you when required information is missing. Plus, you'll receive your results more quickly.

an around-the-world vacation. On paper you have no savings. Yet, when the financial aid officer looks at your income, he or she will think it is very odd that someone who earns a decent living and owns a nice house is so cash poor. This is a red flag, and you'll need to provide additional information. Not only would the financial aid officer not give more financial aid but you would also have no money left to pay for college even if you wanted to.

Financial aid officers are experts at reading financial statements. Just by looking at your 1099 interest reports they can get an accurate estimate of the size of your assets. Trying to trick the college will only backfire. Financial aid officers are professionals who have seen every trick in the book. Our best advice on trickery is to not attempt it.

525.

How your financial aid is packaged makes a difference

Let's assume that your Expected Family Contribution is lower than the cost of one year in college and therefore you have financial need. Once that amount is determined it is up to the financial aid office at the college to try to put together a package that will meet that need. The college may not always be able to do it and unless it is the college's policy to meet all financial need of its students, then the college is under no obligation to provide anything. Of course, most colleges will try.

The way in which your aid is packaged will differ not only because your financial need changes with the price of each college but also because colleges have varying amounts of financial aid resources. The following is a detailed description of what you might find in your aid package. Most financial aid packages consist of a combination of these sources.

526. Federal Pell Grants
These grants are for undergraduate study for students who have the most financial need, typically with Expected Family Contributions of $5,487 or less. The amount varies based on your EFC, but the maximum amount for the 2018-19 school year is $6,095. All students who apply for financial aid by completing the FAFSA and are determined to have financial need by their college will be considered for Federal Pell Grants.

527. Federal Supplemental Educational Opportunity Grants
These grants are for undergraduates with the most financial need. The government provides limited funds for individual schools to administer this program. This means there is no guarantee that every eligible student will receive an FSEOG Grant. The amount varies between $100 and $4,000 per year, and the specific amount is determined by the college on a case by case basis.

528. Grants from the college
The college itself has various need-based and merit-based grants. By applying for financial aid you will be considered for these grants.

529. State grants
Your state may offer both need and merit-based grants. While some grants are administered by the state, others are distributed to the colleges to administer.

530. Federal Work-Study
Work-study provides jobs for undergraduate and graduate students with financial need allowing you to earn money while attending school. The focus is on providing work experience in your area of study. Generally, you will work for your school on campus or for a non-profit organization or public agency if you work off campus. You will have a limit on the hours you can work in this program. Your wages are based on the federal minimum wage although it is usually higher.

531. State Work-Study

Besides the federal program, some states also have a work-study program that mirrors the operation of the federal program.

532. Subsidized and Unsubsidized Federal Direct Loans

There are two types of Direct Loans: Subsidized Direct Loans and Unsubsidized Direct Loans. The U.S. government is the lender. You can borrow up to $5,500 as a freshman (with up to $3,500 of this amount subsidized), $6,500 as a sophomore (with up to $4,500 of this amount subsidized) and $7,500 as a junior or senior dependent undergraduate student (with up to $5,500 of this amount subsidized). If your parents are denied a parent loan or you are an independent student, the school may offer loans of up to $9,500 for freshmen (with up to $3,500 of this amount subsidized), $10,500 for sophomores (up to $4,500 subsidized) and $12,500 for junior and seniors (up to $5,500 subsidized).

Depending on your financial need you may be offered a subsidized or unsubsidized Direct Loan. When the loan is subsidized the government pays for the interest that accrues while you are in college and before you start to repay it. For unsubsidized loans you must pay the interest that accrues while you are in college although you don't start making any payments until after you graduate from college. For more detailed information about student loans, see Chapter 12.

As a high school student, where can I get my basic questions answered by a financial aid officer?

If you don't want to call a financial aid officer, visit the website of the National Association of Student Financial Aid Administrators. This is a professional organization whose members are college financial aid officers. The website has lots of helpful articles and checklists and information on College Goal Sunday, a free annual program to help students complete the FAFSA. Visit the NASFAA website at http://www.nasfaa.org.

Step 5: Compare And Accept Your Financial Aid

A few weeks after you receive your acceptance letters from the colleges you will also get your financial aid award letters. These letters will outline the specific types and dollar amounts that each college is offering. You should compare these award letters and keep the following tips in mind:

533.

You can pick and choose which parts of your financial aid package to accept

When you receive an offer of financial aid you don't have to accept or reject the whole package. You are free to pick and choose the specific pieces of aid you want. If you are offered a grant you'll definitely want to accept it, but you might not want to accept the loan component. When you are analyzing your award package consider each piece separately.

534.

If you need more don't be shy to ask for a re-evaluation

If you feel that the amount of financial aid that you are offered by a college is simply nowhere near enough, you can ask for a re-evaluation. For the re-evaluation to be effective you need to provide the financial aid office with concrete reasons why their initial assessment was wrong. Start with a letter or call to the financial aid office. Be sure that you have all of your documents ready, and remember that the squeaky wheel gets the grease. If you don't say anything about your package the college will assume that you are happy with it. We have a special chapter that is dedicated to asking for a re-evaluation. See Chapter 9 for more details.

535.

Don't lose your financial aid

All financial aid comes with the stipulation that you maintain "satisfactory academic progress." This means that you need to take a minimum number of classes per semester and must have passing grades. If you drop too many classes or take too long to graduate you could jeopardize not only your chances of ever getting a diploma but also your financial aid package.

Asking For More Financial Aid

How To Ask For More Money

Let's get one thing out of the way. College financial aid officers hate the word "negotiate." Perhaps it's because the word conjures up images of haggling with a car salesperson over the cost of floor mats. But regardless of the word you use, it is a well-documented fact that colleges do have wiggle room when it comes to your financial aid package. If you approach them in the right way and provide the right evidence, you may be able to lower the sticker price of your education.

But if you can't use the word "negotiate," what do you call bargaining with the colleges? The word that financial aid officers don't mind is "reassessment." Basically this means you ask the financial aid officers to reconsider the financial aid package that they offered you. But you can't just ask for a reassessment without a reason. You need to provide financial aid officers with concrete reasons for why you deserve a better financial aid package.

If you look at a typical financial aid offer you'll notice that there are two critical areas that determine how much you get.

1. Your Expected Family Contribution. This is the amount that the college has determined that your family can afford to pay. They arrive at this figure by crunching the numbers that you provide on your financial aid application. Once the college determines how much you can pay, all they need to figure out is how to make up for the gap between what you can pay and what it costs to attend their college.

2. The packaging of your award. Your financial aid offer might consist of a combination of grants, work-study and student loans. The composition of your award—called packaging—makes a big difference. Would you rather get $10,000 in grants or $10,000 in student loans?

Your goal when asking for a "reassessment" is to provide reasons for why the Expected Family Contribution is not accurate and makes it extremely difficult or even impossible for you to afford college and/or to increase the amount of grant money in your package. You do this by submitting a letter or scheduling an in-person appointment with the financial aid officer. In your letter or meeting you request a reassessment and provide reasons why the original offer is just not realistic.

The success of your reassessment will depend on the reasons that you give to support your claim that their initial analysis needs fixing. Let's look at some reasons that you can provide to the financial aid office to convince them that they should reassess your financial aid package.

536.

Present any special circumstances not reflected by the numbers in your financial aid application

All the college sees are the numbers that you provide on your financial aid forms. These numbers are based on your income taxes, which are always two years behind. If something has changed recently that affects your family's finances you need to tell the college. Changes to your family's finances may include:

- Unusual medical expenses
- Tuition for a sibling including private secondary or elementary school expenses
- Unemployment of a spouse or parent
- Ongoing divorce or separation
- Care for an aging relative

Whatever the circumstance be sure to explain it in detail in your letter or when you meet with the financial aid officer. Don't just describe the event, but show with numbers how it impacts your family's finances. Financial aid officers like to deal with numbers, which means you need to justify everything with them.

537.

Don't wait for something bad to happen if you know it will

You don't have to wait until something happens to let the financial aid officer know about it. If you know that there will be a change in your parents' employment or if there will be an unavoidable financial expenditure, let the financial aid office know about it now. Like any large organization the college has a limited budget. If you wait until something happens it might be too late for the college to do anything about it. If you let them know in advance they may be able to budget for it and have the money for you when the inevitable occurs.

538.

Play one college off another college

If you have been accepted to several colleges and receive financial aid packages that are vastly different, you may be able to use one to motivate the other to be a little more generous. Let's imagine that your first choice, College A, gives you a smaller aid package or one that is composed of only loans. Not a very attractive offer. However, your second choice, College B, gives you either a bigger package or more of your money in grants. Now you are in a position to ask College A to match the offer of College B.

First, email a letter to College A. Begin by stating that you are extremely excited about being accepted and would very much like to attend the college. Explain that given the financial aid package offered, you may not be able to afford the costs. Justify in real numbers why their offer is not sufficient. This, of course, must be true since the college can see all of your family's finances. Not wanting to spend your money is not a good reason. Not having the money to spend is an excellent reason. There is a big difference between the two.

After you make a case for why you need more financial aid, share the better offer made by College B. Include a copy of the award letter

> **How should I contact the financial aid office to ask for a reassessment?**
>
> If you are a high school senior, time is of the essence since you receive admission offers in April and often have to make a decision by May. Even if you are already in college, timing is important because financial aid budgets do get depleted. If you are close to the college, you should try to make an in-person appointment. Otherwise, go with email. Sending snail mail just takes too long. You need to give the college time to respond, so the sooner you can let them know of your request for a reassessment the better.

from College B with your letter. Point out to the financial aid officer that given the generous package from College B it makes it hard to turn down. Politely reiterate that you would prefer to attend College A and would like to know if there is anything the financial aid office can do to reassess your aid package.

Throughout the letter you want to be friendly and polite. Remember you are not negotiating for a lower price on a car but asking for a reassessment and providing another college's better offer (as well as your own family's finances) as a basis. You want to avoid sounding confrontational or argumentative. You also need to have concrete reasons why you need more financial aid.

This technique does not guarantee success. In fact, no college is under any obligation to change its original offer. However, if you can present a compelling case, you may find that the college is willing to reassess the initial offer and adjust the aid package. You only want to do this with the college you really want to attend. Don't try to pit a whole bunch of colleges against each other. It will only backfire. Focus on your first choice college, and try to use the better offer of your second choice as leverage. If it doesn't work, you can always attend your second choice college, which offered you the better package.

539.

Be polite and never threaten

Some parents take an aggressive approach to asking for more. This rarely works. Financial aid officers are professionals who believe in the aid package that they have created. They know they are not beyond making mistakes and are happy to take a second look if you present a good reason to do so. However, if you come across as aggressive, abrasive or confrontational, they will have little desire to help.

540.

Have a number in mind

When you present your case to the financial aid officer her or she may surprise you by asking: "So, how much do you need?" This is not the time to be tongue-tied! Have the amount you need in mind!

541.

Always, always be honest

During the entire financial aid process you must be honest. If you try to hide, exaggerate or outright lie about your circumstances you will not only lose any change of getting more aid but you will also be subjected to stiff fines and even jail time. Being dishonest on a financial aid application is the same as cheating on your taxes and carries similar federal penalties. On the other hand, as mentioned earlier don't be modest about your financial problems. Don't hide embarrassing facts such as bad credit that prevents you from taking out a loan. The financial aid officer has seen and heard it all and really does want to help.

542.

Example of a successful financial aid reassessment

You can ask for a reassessment at any time during college when something changes in your family's finances. The following is an actual letter one student wrote to the Harvard financial aid office. Before writing the letter, the student had received only a small loan from Harvard despite the fact that her father had been laid off for over a year. The student composed this letter to explain her family's extenuating circumstances, describing their actual income and expenses. Notice how she substantiates her claims with real dollar examples. Her letter paid off–she got a $6,500 grant per semester for the rest of the year!

Dear Sir or Madam:

I am writing to request that my financial aid package for the fall semester be reconsidered. My family and I were disappointed with the amount we were offered because in addition to my father having been unemployed for over a year, my older sister will be a sophomore in college, and my mother, a part-time teacher, has received no income since June because of summer break.

We understand that nearly every family must undergo an amount of hardship to send its members to college. However, because my parents wish to continue financing my sister's and my education, they are worried about how they will pay for their own expenses. They have been using my mother's income to basically cover their mortgage payments and their savings to pay for everything else. In February, my parents had $33,000 in savings. In the last six months, their savings has decreased by about $15,000. They now have about $18,000 to contribute to my sister's and my college expenses as well as to spend on their and my younger brother's food and basic necessities. They don't know how long their savings will last without a change in the amount of aid I will receive.

At the end of this month, my sister will begin her sophomore year at USC. The cost will be $74,825, and she has received $63,510 in financial aid. One of the things you might be able to address is why my sister's financial aid package was dramatically higher than mine.

Since July of last year my father has been unemployed. His severance pay ended in October, and his unemployment benefits have been depleted since February.

Although he has applied for over a dozen positions, his prospects for finding a job in his specialty are slim.

My parents and I have discussed the possibility of having me take a year off so that I may work to help pay for tuition, but we'd much rather that I finish school now and work after I have received my degree.

Please contact my parents or me with any further questions you may have. Thank you very much for your time and consideration. I hope that this information is helpful in your review of my application.

Sincerely Yours,

There's no guarantee that a letter like this will work, but if the financial situation of your family changes significantly and you can show with numbers how it has affected your ability to pay, you need to get in touch with your financial aid office. There is absolutely no harm in asking.

Avoid Financial Aid Scams

Keeping Your Money Safe

An important part of saving money for college is keeping your hard-earned cash out of the hands of scam artists. Recently, the Federal Trade Commission reported that there were over 175,000 incidents of financial aid scams, which cost consumers more than $25 million. This represents only the scams that were reported, and we've met hundreds of families that have gotten taken for varying amounts from $20 to more than $1,000 who never reported the incident.

To keep your money safe you need to know what to watch out for in a scam. Most scams begin in the same way. An offer arrives in an official looking envelope from a company with an equally official sounding name. Inside you usually find a letter that appeals to your fear on how you are going to pay for college. Then it makes an almost unbelievable offer. For a small sum of money this company will help you locate unclaimed scholarships, maximize your financial aid package and help you pay for college without any financial pain. It offers the answer you have been looking for and the price is peanuts compared to what you were planning to shell out for tuition.

If you send in a check you have probably just become another statistic for the Federal Trade Commission. We should point out that not all of these offers are illegal, which helps to explain why they exist year after year. But they certainly don't live up to their promises. Often what you get for your money is usually much less than you expected and certainly not worth your hard earned money.

To keep your money safe, you need to understand the difference between what is promised and what you actually will receive. Let's take a look at how some of these scams work and why you should avoid them.

543.

The hook: For a fee we will find "hidden" scholarships that nobody knows about. This virtually guarantees that you will be a winner.

The reality: For all practical purposes there is no such thing as a "hidden" scholarship. There are some obscure scholarships that have criteria that almost nobody can meet so they do go un-awarded. But chances are if 99.99 percent of students can't meet the criteria to enter then neither will you. All legitimate scholarships that have reasonable eligibility requirements go awarded. It is true that some have very few applicants, but these are not the awards that you will get. What you will typically receive is a generic list of scholarships that are anything but hidden or a list of scholarships that have such specific criteria that nobody can qualify.

544.

The hook: To enter our mucho-money scholarship you must pay a tiny application fee. After all, what's $5 or $10 to enter if you can walk away with $1,000 or more in scholarships?

The reality: After paying the fee and sending in the application you'll get a nice card that says, "Sorry but you are not a winner." These companies count on tens of thousands of students sending in the application fee. Then even if they have to randomly award a $1,000 scholarship they still bank a huge sum of money from the fees. The defense against these kinds of fake scholarships is simple: Never pay an application fee. Real scholarships do not require any fee from applicants. Scholarship organizations, after all, are trying to give money away, not take it from those who apply. If a scholarship organization can't afford to process applications without a fee then they have no business giving away a scholarship.

The one exception is for a competition where it is more common to include a fee with your submission, but these are usually limited to musical or artistic compositions and performances. Plus, these competitions are not technically scholarships so our rule is still true: Never pay an entry or application fee for a scholarship.

545.

The hook: You've won our scholarship! All we need is your credit card number to verify your eligibility so we can send you the money.

The reality: You'll get some unexpected and unwanted charges on your credit card. Never give out your credit card information to a scholarship organization.

546.

The hook: We guarantee that you will win at least one scholarship!

The reality: There is no such thing as a guaranteed scholarship. Scholarships are competitive and by definition not every applicant will win. The only way you would have a "guaranteed win" is if you had to pay an entry fee and the prize you won was less than what you paid, but we don't think any of you feel like paying $500 to be a guaranteed winner of a $100 scholarship.

547.

The hook: For a fee we will help you complete the FAFSA application and submit it for you.

The reality: The full name of the FAFSA is the Free Application for Federal Student Aid. Notice how the word free is right there at the beginning. The FAFSA is designed to be completed by students and parents. Now, this is not to say that it is easy. It is similar to doing your taxes and in fact much of the information from your 1040 will be used to complete the FAFSA. However, to pay a company a fee to complete